ORNAMENT
IS NOT A CRIME

Rebecca L Gross

ORNAMENT IS NOT A CRIME

Contemporary interiors
with a postmodern twist

T&H

CONTENTS

~

6

INTRODUCTION

~~~~~~

Modernist architects and designers of the 20th century lived and designed by some hard-and-fast rules: 'form follows function', 'less is more' and 'ornament is a crime'. While these architectural creeds resulted in striking modern buildings and spaces, they left little room for expression, diversity or informality. Emerging in the 1960s and hitting their stride from the 1970s through to the early 1990s, postmodern architects and designers rebelled against modernism's utopian ideals and stifling rules and rationality. Breaking free from formality and seriousness, they created fresh, provocative designs across architecture, furniture, lamps, mirrors, homewares and more.

Colour, pattern, materials, ornament and motifs were the heroes of postmodern (also known as PoMo) architecture and design. The bigger and brighter the better, but they weren't used without meaning. (In the early stages, at least.) Rather, they appealed to the senses and served as signifiers for function and context; a communicative and emotive language that carried meaning and expression.

Architects and designers challenged traditional forms and functions and added decoration for aesthetic effect. They blurred the lines of high art and popular culture, as well as the hierarchies of 'high' and 'low' materials and 'good' and 'bad' taste. Cheap materials were used to make expensive products, and history and symbolism became a treasure trove of inspiration with nods to classicism, nostalgia and tongue-in-cheek references.

After decades of strict modernism, design could be populist and kitsch, humorous, witty and flippant. And the enduring was eschewed for the ephemeral, as these designers never intended their objects to be part of an everlasting fashion.

As the 1980s progressed, the bold postmodern style became the designer look of the decade, associated with corporate capitalism, conspicuous consumption and excess. And as it trickled down to the mainstream, it became more surface than substance – its ideas and intentions diluted and its forms and ornament merely pastiche.

Becoming misunderstood – even controversial – the postmodern movement was relatively short-lived and by the 1990s, modernism began to dominate again. Contemporary minimalism boomed in the 2000s, accompanied by the mid-century modern revival and the popularity of Scandinavian design. And with it, architecture and interiors began to lose the rich visual expression that was so prevalent in previous decades. But in the same way that postmodernism followed modernism, the themes behind PoMo are emerging again, hot on the heels of minimalism.

The interiors, furniture and objects featured in this book are contemporary, but they also play with postmodern design themes, sometimes knowingly and literally, and sometimes incidentally. From daring to delightful and wild to wonderful, the homes and pieces here are rich in vitality and meaning.

These twenty-one homes from around the world are an expressive and meaningful part of their residents' identities and lifestyles. Each is a world unto itself, reflective of the clients, the designers and their open-minded and trusting relationship. They are derived from a household's personalities and preferences, rather than based on resale value, and there was often explicit opportunity for architects and designers to explore new ideas, and confidence instilled to follow their intuition. The furniture and objects featured in the five designer profiles also break from conventional design, with forms and functionality reimagined in playful, sensory and refreshing ways.

Previous page: California Bungalow by Ash Dipert (p. 242).
Left: *Elementary Abacus* by Marta Figueiredo (p. 50).

7

Before we view the houses, let's meet a few of the original movers and shakers of postmodernism to uncover some themes.

Postmodernism emerged in different ways across different countries. Some of the key protagonists were in America and Italy, but there were many others across Britain, Europe, Japan and more – Ricardo Bofill, Hans Hollein, Terry Farrell, Kengo Kuma, Aldo Rossi, George Sowden, James Stirling, to name a few.

In America, postmodern architects and designers drew on themes and ornament from historical and vernacular styles. Husband-and-wife architecture duo Robert Venturi and Denise Scott Brown were influential theorists and practitioners of postmodernism, before architectural historian and cultural theorist Charles Jencks applied the term to architecture in *The Language of Post-Modern Architecture* in 1977. In rebuttal to Ludwig Mies van der Rohe's dictum that 'less is more', Venturi countered 'less is a bore' in his 1966 book *Complexity and Contradiction in Architecture*. He championed architecture that offers depth, meaning and ambiguity and aimed for vitality over unity. Vitality, which Venturi believed should be embraced, not erased by modernist buildings, was later celebrated in *Learning from Las Vegas* (1972), in which Venturi, Scott Brown and architect Steven Izenor investigated the symbolism of architecture and the commercial landscape.

Venturi and Scott Brown designed architecture to be communicative and meaningful, while also championing the ordinary and familiar. They used recognisable architectural elements, like a gable and chimney, to signify a house; and classical features, such as columns and pediments, to indicate important buildings. But their work wasn't in any way ordinary – they embellished their buildings with colour, signs and symbols. One of Venturi's earliest buildings, Vanna Venturi House (Pennsylvania, 1964), is an assembly of geometric forms, with ornamental details that serve little functional purpose other than to make the composition a visual statement. Venturi and Scott Brown's Children's Museum of Houston (Texas, 1992) has a flamboyant, bright yellow, cartoon-like Greek-temple facade that reflects the significance of the building, yet is friendly and playful to appeal to kids. Venturi and Scott Brown also designed a series of chairs for Knoll in 1984, covering abstracted, silhouetted forms of historic furniture styles with lively, colourful patterns and imagery.

Postmodernism predominantly materialised in large-scale architecture in America, such as the Portland Building (Oregon, 1982) by architect and product designer Michael Graves. Wishing to break the modernist homogeneity, he created stylised facades for the Portland Building with reinterpreted classical elements and colour for symbolism. Graves not only embraced colour and motifs to convey information in architecture, he also did this in his product design, as in the Bird Whistle kettle for Alessi (1985) that sings when the water boils and the bread-shaped toaster for JC Penney (2013).

When it came to residential interiors, decking them out in full PoMo was often overkill, so they were more often realised with select elements, such as columns and individual furniture pieces, rather than a fully fledged scheme. That's not to say they didn't exist, though. The pool house designed by architect Robert AM Stern in Llewellyn Park, New Jersey (1982), with its glitzy palm tree columns and Egyptian references, appears '1980s' through and through.

Charles Moore was another postmodern architect who believed buildings could communicate, and his Piazza d'Italia (New Orleans, 1978) is an icon of the movement and style. The memorial and public space reflects Moore's ideas that architecture be inclusive and democratic and inspire delight and joy. Dedicated to the Italian community, the piazza is a theatrical baroque-like display filled with cultural references to Italy, including columns and arches and a tiled, boot-shaped map.

The Italian approach to postmodern design was experimental, radical and subversive. Emerging in the mid-1960s, the Italian Radical Design movement, as it became known, changed the game, as young architects and designers applied their craft with the desire to change the world. Groups such as Archizoom Associati, Superstudio, Studio65 and UFO, supported by manufacturers like Gufram and Poltronova, explored new materials and processes and designed objects that subverted form and function, often with irreverent humour. With a rebellious spirit and revolutionary ideals, these architects and designers wanted to provoke reactions and new behaviours and imagine other ways of living.

8

Right: Ettore Sottsass's *Tahiti* table lamp for the Memphis Group (1981). in LA Residence by Chet Architecture and Ghislaine Viñas (p. 146).

Following page: Rolf's Apartment by Studio Job (p. 120).

Archizoom's Safari sofa (1967) has scalloped, upholstered seats and backrests in a form and pattern influenced by pop art. Studio65's Capitello chair (1979) adapts a Greek Ionic capital and column into a seat and used cheap polyurethane foam as a substitute for marble. Gufram's Pratone Green (1971) brings the outside world inside. Its long, green stalks – like a giant patch of grass – form an unconventional lounging solution.

Architect and designer Ettore Sottsass was an influential figure, already on the scene. He was a design consultant for Olivetti and an artistic director for Poltronova, where he developed bold, colourful and sculptural objects like the wavy, neon Ultrafragola mirror (1970), which is again taking pride of place in many homes. His designs were based on the idea that the world is perceived through the senses, and he emphasised the sensorial rather than the structural aspects of his pieces.

In the late 1970s, Sottsass, along with designers Andrea Branzi, Michele De Lucchi, Alessandro Mendini, Paola Navone and others, contributed work to the experimental Studio Alchimia, founded by Alessandro Guerriero in 1976. The group reworked famous objects as critiques of good design. Mendini became a prominent proponent of the group with his reinterpretations of classic and modernist furniture and his interest in surface treatment for aesthetic appeal. He abstracted the form of a Biedermeier sofa and decorated it with brightly painted abstract shapes to create the Kandissi sofa (1979), and covered an ornate Rococo revival chair with a colourful confetti of pointillist brushstrokes to create the Proust armchair (1979).

In 1981, Mendini, Sottsass, Branzi, De Lucchi, plus other designers, including Nathalie Du Pasquier and Barbara Radice formed the Memphis Group (also known as Memphis Milano or simply Memphis), taking their name from the Bob Dylan song 'Stuck Inside of Mobile with the Memphis Blues Again'. While Memphis was short-lived, disbanding in 1987, it electrified the design world with its intriguing and idiosyncratic pieces that included furniture, lighting, fabrics, carpets, ceramics, glass and metal objects and appealed to people on an emotional level.

The Memphis Group shocked and bemused visitors and media when it debuted its first collection at the Salone del Mobile in Milan in 1981. The designers used inexpensive and then-unconventional materials for furniture, such as plastic and laminate, pairing exuberant and discordant colours and wild and clashing patterns. They assembled geometric forms into novel and asymmetric compositions, giving their pieces a spirited character and challenging what objects could be. Sottsass gave his Carlton bookshelf/room divider and Casablanca bookcase a robotic character through angular elements, while De Lucchi imbued his Kristall side table and Oceanic table lamp with playful, anthropomorphic expression.

In recent years, the cyclical tides of design have seen a resurgence in the popularity of postmodernism and the work of the Memphis Group and other architects and designers. And as they demonstrated, form doesn't have to follow function, less is not more and ornament is not a crime. Rather architecture and design can be a vehicle of expression and communication and a way to incite happiness and joy.

Likewise, the architects and designers in this book have created interiors and objects that transform the ordinary and everyday with bold colours and patterns, the celebration of surfaces and the juxtaposition of materials. There are twists and plays on shape, scale and form, and expressive and symbolic references, as well as a good dose of wit and whimsy. But as the original postmodernists knew, this is not without meaning. These strong concepts are driven by personalities, preferences, interests and memories, all imagined in vibrant and expressive ways to infuse our homes and lives with richness, vitality and meaning.

11

LET'S DANCE

~~~

Designer: Owl Design
Project name: Adventures in Space
Location: London, United Kingdom

Photographer: Rachael Smith

When an apartment offers sweeping city views, the client brief is often for a design that draws your attention outdoors. Here, it's what's on the inside that matters. 'Our client's brief was to design an interior more eye-catching than the apartment's views,' says designer Simone Gordon. To compete with the panorama of London's cityscape and the River Thames, Owl Design played with shapes, forms and colour to create a fun, adventurous space that engages you from the first steps through the door.

The London apartment is the city pad and second home of a musician. Located in a curving, sculptural building by Foster + Partners, it was formerly a bland and beige show home with little style or personality. This provided a blank canvas for Owl, as did the brief from the client, who wanted to use their second home for hosting friends and entertaining. 'They had confidence in us and we were very free to go wild with it, which was an absolute dream,' says designer Sophie van Winden. Owl took inspiration from the building's form and the view, as well as a book about the Memphis Group and the client's artwork of David Bowie (who was also a fan and collector of Memphis) to create something refreshing and new. 'We looked at everything but the mainstream design you see out there at the moment,' says Simone.

The Bowie artwork is the main attraction in the hallway. The mosaic of broken CDs combines cool blues and warm reds, which Owl continued throughout the home, also inspired by the view. Cornflower blue draws in the colour of the sky, gentle minty green evokes the oxidised rooftops and orange and red nods to the surrounding buildings.

Strong geometries and patterns are at play throughout the living area. The flowing form of the building and the River Thames are echoed in the curved walls and the snaking sofa, custom designed like a tête-à-tête (seating with backrests that face in opposite directions, for easy conversation). In contrast, sharp triangles prevail in the joinery wall, rectangles radiate from the circular rug and blue, grey and black shapes are scattered across the Marmoleum flooring designed by Owl. 'The project started when the 2020 lockdown happened, so it was quite indulgent for us and the client budget allowed for nearly everything in the apartment to be bespoke and custom designed,' says Simone. This includes the drinks cabinet, with its fluted doors and sculpted blue handles that open to a coral-coloured surprise.

Textured surfaces infuse warmth and tactility into the cool palette, with Venetian plaster finish on the living and dining area walls, framed pieces of embossed wallpaper in the hallway and patterned timber panelling in the snug. This room has a loungey 1970s vibe – plush carpet, a velvet sofa and deep-purple wall panelling enhance the acoustics and cosiness of the room.

The client wanted all three bedrooms to feel like they belonged in a boutique hotel. Each one has its own look, while staying on theme with the colour palette, geometric patterns and curved headboard. In the toilet, it's disco all the way. When you open the door, 'Let's Dance' by David Bowie plays on loop and a mirror ball illuminates the glittering sequined walls.

'A home should make you happy and it should mirror your personality,' says Sophie. Designed with attention to what's on the inside, rather than outside, this apartment is the embodiment of the courage to be adventurous and different.

14

Previous page: A customised painting by LRNCE takes centre stage between the kitchen and dining area.
Right: The mosaic artwork of David Bowie inspired the cool blue and warm red colour palette.

Following page: Owl designed bespoke pieces throughout the apartment, including the shelving, cabinetry, Hux dining table, Forbo flooring and Reese rug.

Left: The fluted doors of the drinks cabinet open to reveal its coral-coloured interior.

Above: Owl Design's bespoke curved sofa and Varier's Ekstrem chair have sculptural lines that contrast with the strong geometric forms in the room.

Above, left to right: Guest bedroom with lamp from OYOY and black-and-white vase by Lydia Hardwock; Main bedroom with bespoke side tables and headboard by Owl Design.

Right: Guest bedroom with geometric patterns on the curtains and Arte wallpaper.

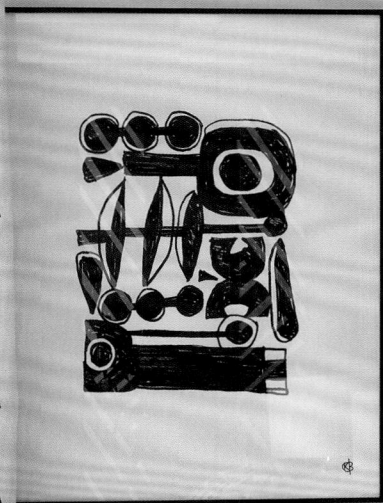

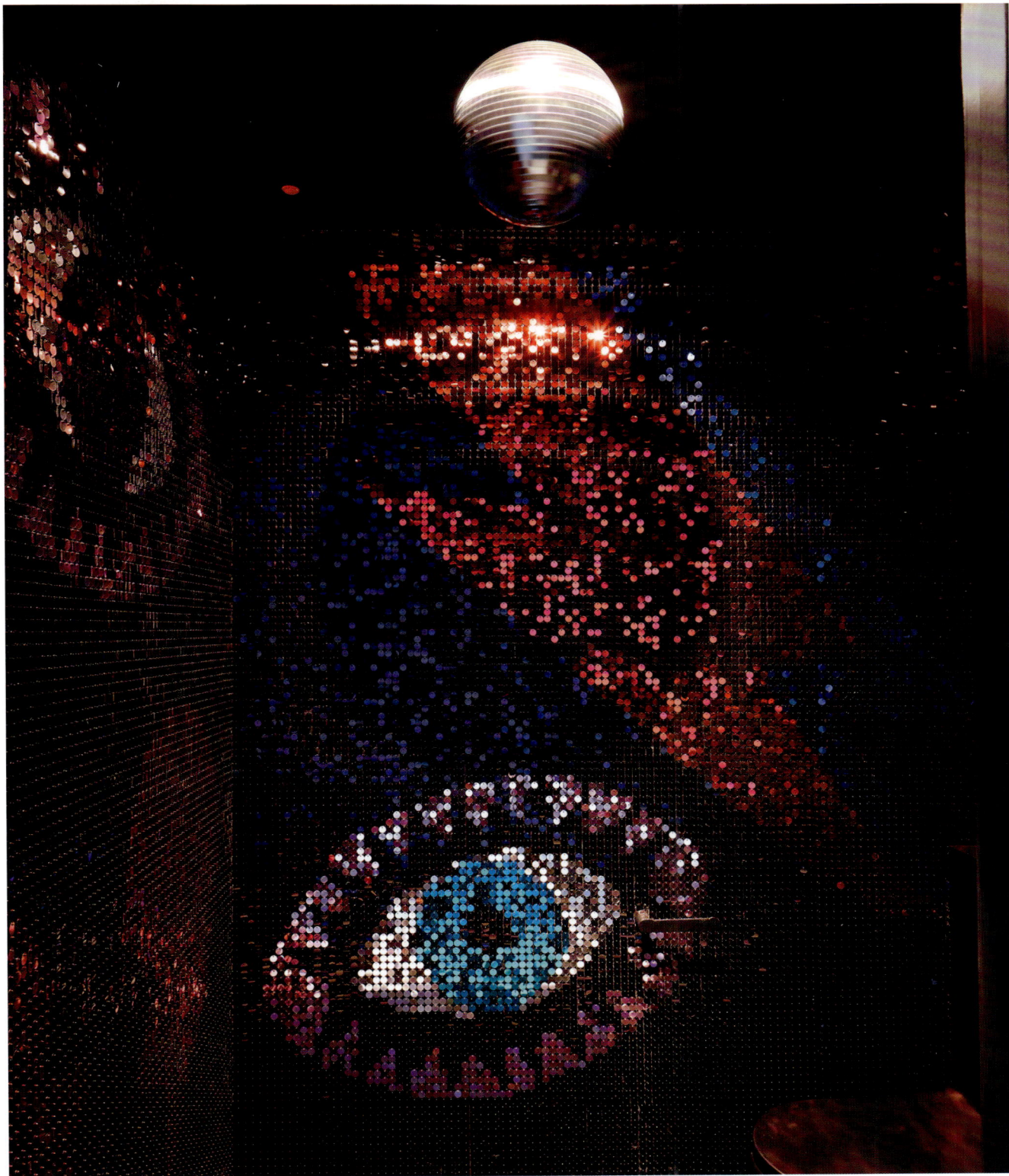

Left: A velvet-upholstered sofa and deep-purple wall panelling provide a cosy atmosphere in the snug.

Above: A mirror ball illuminates the sequin-covered walls.
Following page: In the hallway is a HK Living Console table with Porta Romana wall lights and Reflections Copenhagen mirror.

'Because so many people have access to interior design images, a lot of things start being the same. This project allowed us to explore our own creativity and to create something one-off.'

Simone Gordon,
co-founder and designer, Owl Design

Owl Design

FEARLESS EXPRESSION

~~~

Designer: YSG
Project name: Polychrome House
Location: Sydney, Australia

Photographer: Prue Ruscoe
Colour consulting and mural: Lymesmith

Emotion and energy are driving forces in YSG's approach to design, and this is visible in the fresh and fearless strokes of bold colour and graphic materials of Polychrome House in Sydney. 'My process starts with imagining how I want a space to feel – its mood, its attitude, its references. I work subliminally, striving for an emotional outcome,' says designer Yasmine Ghoniem.

The owners are a couple of art lovers with three children and their brief to YSG was challenging. Functionally, they wanted to transform their 1960s two-bedroom, two-bathroom brick house into a home with three bedrooms, three bathrooms, an integrated indoor/outdoor retreat and a large living area. Aesthetically and atmospherically, they wanted the brick interior to 'blossom into an energetic design playground bursting with colour. A place that accelerated their mood the moment they entered,' says Yasmine.

YSG moved the kitchen to the ground floor and expanded the living area, removing the rear facade of the house to open it to the outdoors and the jungle-like view. A third bedroom, ensuite and loft was built upstairs, where the kitchen used to be. The existing brown brick and painted timber interior provided a giant canvas, which YSG and local design practice Lymesmith transformed with a vibrant and expressive palette. Quiet neutrals and soft pastels are punctuated with bold, bright colours that draw attention to feature walls and furniture items.

The floor is animated with a graphic pattern of black slate crazy pavers that connect indoors and out and reference the original era of the house. Sections of brick and timber provide an earthy and textural accompaniment to the primary colours and pastel hues injected throughout like an abstract painting.

An abstract mural is the focal point of the living area. Lymesmith painted the wall with a composition inspired by aerial photographs of the property's bayside location. 'The mural, with its zigzags, angles and squiggles and potent mix of primary colours, is pure Memphis in 2D,' says Yasmine. Lymesmith also painted a mural on the entry wall, with abstract white boats bobbing along the coastline and ocean. Classic pieces of mid-century furniture add to the dollops of colour and forms, and enhance the cheerful spirit of the house.

A custom brick plinth with seat pads separates the living area from the kitchen, where the joinery wall is bright yellow, the rear wall is painted terracotta red and a long black scrawl runs through the marble splashback, mimicking the crazy paving. 'It looks like an expressive gesture drawn by an artist, or like a bolt of energy charging the home.'

Mushroom-pink carpet covers the stairs, and white cork tiles replace shag pile floors on the first storey. The same colour palette is used upstairs, where more subdued tones and shades of green complement the treetop views. YSG also stripped back the plasterboard ceiling to its timber battens to enhance the space and light, replaced the enclosed wooden balustrades with flat bars and inserted colourful timber dowels to separate bedrooms and ensuites to ensure natural light flowed through.

Polychrome House is an uplifting and happy home that reflects the family's desire for joyful living. Intended to be their 'forever' home, the house embraces colour and personality, favouring energy, emotion and self-expression.

Previous page: Black slate crazy pavers provide an animated backdrop to Andreu World's Reverse dining table and Pierre Paulin's Groovy chair in purple.

Right: In the upstairs living area, the green tones in the rug, sofa and chair harmonise with nature outdoors.

Above: The mural by Lymesmith is inspired by aerial photographs of the property's bayside location.

Right: The kitchen and living area are separated by a custom brick plinth with seat pads.
Following page: Yellow, red and blue provide bold tonal highlights against the black slate, timber, brick and marble in the kitchen.

34

'Like the Memphis Group's approach,
my process is as much about
an attitude as it is aesthetic.
This project definitely draws upon
the lust for colour and bold shapes
and there's no denying abstract
expressionism's loose brush strokes
also played a subliminal role.'

Yasmine Ghoniem,
director and designer, YSG

Previous page: Lymesmith's abstract yellow mural on the entry wall is of white boats bobbing along the coastline and ocean.

Above left to right: Brickwork provides a warm textural feature to the subdued palette of the bedroom; A loft with study maximises a small space. Right: Colourful timber dowels separate bedrooms and ensuites.

FRESH FLAVOUR

~~~

Architect/designer: WOWOWA
Project name: Pony
Location: Melbourne, Australia

Photographer: Martina Gemmola
Stylist: Ruth Welsby

A bright yellow door with a porthole window gives you a taste of the playful interior that lies behind the facade of Pony, a 1960s apricot-brick home in Melbourne. The owners who engaged WOWOWA had open minds about their renovation and were attracted to the studio because of its fun, fresh and imaginative style. 'The personality and aesthetic of the family heavily inspired the design, and we brought it alive through form, materiality and colour,' says architect Monique Woodward.

The clients needed additional space for their vibrant and energetic family of six. WOWOWA designed a modest addition and reconfigured internal spaces to create different zones, a sense of separation and better outdoor connections. The addition was layered with colours, details and references to the residents' lives and the heritage and context of the house. 'We pull the context apart, find the playfulness and then reassemble it on steroids. We find the fruit in the tree and then really riff on it,' Monique explains.

The kitchen is the cornerstone of the house, opening to the dining and living area that has views of the front garden, back garden and pool. The sitting room and the parents' bedroom and ensuite extend from one side of the kitchen, and the children's bedrooms are on the other side, providing separate zones. The passage along the children's wing is a 'clip-on colonnade', with a rhythmic pattern of columns and windows that open to an outlook of the garden and pool. A daybed is bathed in sun at the end of the colonnade, and a bookshelf and two breakout areas provide different places for the children to play. 'It is an accretion of small moments of delight.'

The crafted undulating roof is another moment of delight, casting a scalloped shadow down the brick wall. This house is near a beach, and WOWOWA took inspiration from the construction of a boat, expressing the 'keel' down the length of the colonnade. Nautical references continue in the porthole windows, brass fittings and timber decking on the floor and curved ceiling. The curved form is repeated in the arched doorway between the parents' bedroom and bathroom, and in the children's painted wardrobes. 'For us, ornament is not a crime. Ornament is architectural, and the layering of ornamentation changes the way you perceive and experience a space. Life is too short for boring spaces,' says Monique.

A celebration of what WOWOWA calls 'story-in-place' is at the heart of the studio's design process. It's about embedding the owners' nostalgic memories and special experiences into their home through colours, materials and forms. A case in point is the kitchen benchtops in banana yellow that evoke Paddle Pop ice creams, a reminder of childhood days. A palette of confectionery colours reigns throughout the kitchen – fairy floss–pink cabinetry, rich chocolate-brown timber joinery and speckled terrazzo floor and splashback. The bedrooms, bathrooms and joinery have delicious fruity hues with playful pairings of raspberry, peach, tangerine, grape, lemon, blueberry, pink and green.

Original door handles have been kept and reused, drawing attention to what might not have been seen before. 'We like to embellish the original and highlight the forgotten elements. It gives them a new life and they can be read in a different way.'

By having fun with the design, WOWOWA has created a family home that exudes vitality and delight. Through meaningful plays on materiality, form and colour, Pony captures the personality and story of the family who live in it.

40

Previous page: A daybed at the end of the passageway provides a space to read and relax in the sun.

Right: The 'clip-on colonnade' offers different places for the children to play and features Fearon's Chub stool in green (p. 144).

42

Left: The undulating roof, inspired by the construction of a boat, casts a scalloped shadow down the brick wall.
Above, left to right: The bright yellow door hints at the playful interior; Large glass doors open the kitchen and dining area to the garden.

Following page: The kitchen has a dessert-inspired colour palette with HI-MACS 'Banana' benchtops, Dulux 'Helena Rose' cabinetry, dark brown joinery and Signorino terrazzo tiles.

Above: A pair of children's bedrooms have playful colour combinations that give each room its own personality.

Right: Calm tones and materials offer respite in the main bedroom.
Following page: Blue and orange are a striking combination in the bathroom.

'WOWOWA's engagement with heritage is to smother it, butter it up, be referential. We conserve the original by embellishing it in such a way that it becomes radical.'

Monique Woodward,
director and architect, WOWOWA

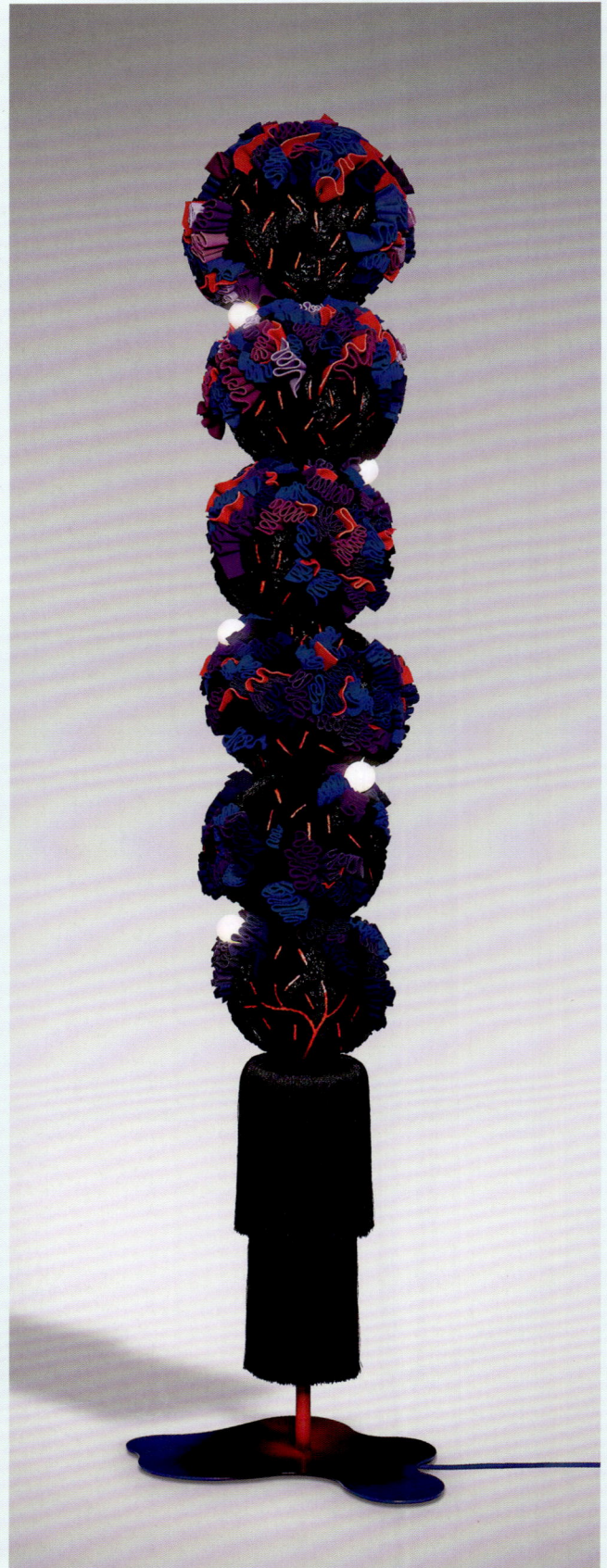

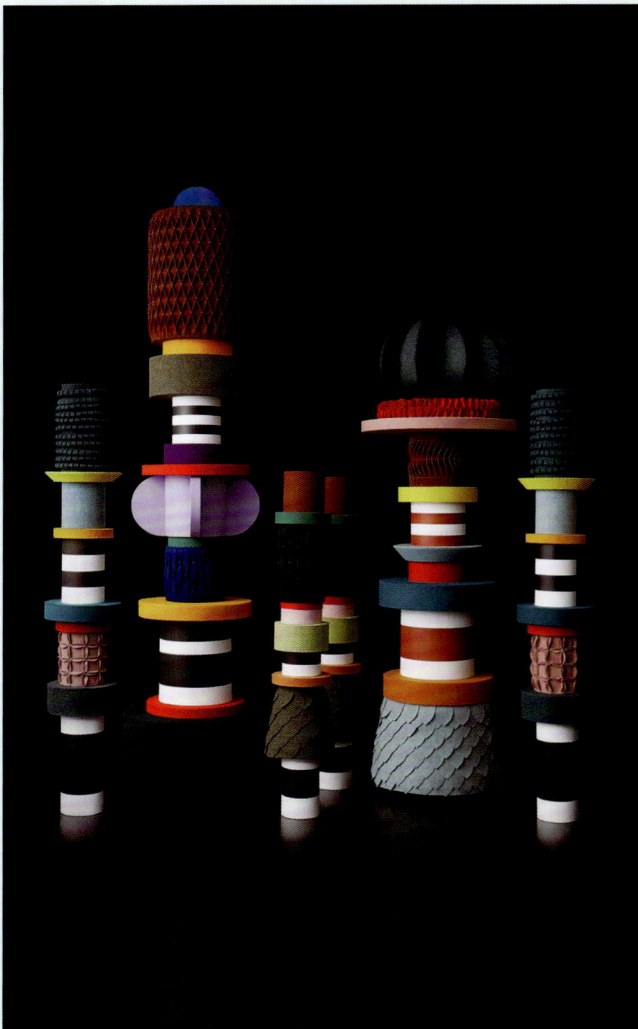

LARGER-THAN-LIFE CREATIONS

~~~

Designer: Marta Figueiredo
Location: Melbourne, Australia

Marta Figueiredo's architectural and anthropomorphic objects provoke joy and delight in people, enticing them to interact, engage and play. But beneath the colourful, tactile, geometric forms, the design of each object is driven by an exploration of topical themes, such as sustainability and inclusivity, and the desire to express a point of view. 'I'm intrigued by the idea of pushing the boundaries of what an object is traditionally thought to be, and I am particularly interested in elements that contribute to a more rich and layered interaction between the individual and the object,' says Marta.

Marta is an architect and multidisciplinary artist, hailing from Portugal and living in Australia. The Prima Familia series of larger-than-life totems emerged from Marta's desire to use burel, a traditional, artisanal Portuguese fabric made from sheep wool. The local burel factories were recently revived and the vivid colours and tactile surfaces sparked her imagination.

Inspired by Oskar Schlemmer's costumes for *The Triadic Ballet*, performed at the Bauhaus in 1922, Marta conceived the totems with scale and proportions that abstract the human form. Performance was a fun and improvisational side of the famous avant-garde Bauhaus school – it was a place to play, experiment further and to free the spirit. 'I was particularly drawn to Johannes Itten's maxim about play being regarded as fundamental for creative thinking. 'Play becomes party – party becomes work – work becomes play,' says Marta, quoting Itten. 'I am a big fan of free-spirited thinking and the Italian Radicals, Situationists and even the Dadaists thought outside the systems and the rules via play.'

Marta expanded Prima Familia with the addition of the Cossack and Queen. Their exaggerated forms, flamboyant colour and three-dimensional surfaces prompting people to touch, feel and even hug the totems. 'I was surprised with what I gave life to, and the emotional connection people have with them.'

This emotional connection inspired Marta to think about the relationships people have with objects, and specifically about her sister who is autistic. She then created Elementary Abacus, a giant toy and side table with movable, musical and sensorial elements that offers an animated and inclusive way of interacting with a piece of furniture.

The conceptual narratives of Marta's designs originate from a topic, question or moment in time. Her latest totem, Creatures of Light, is an illuminated sculpture about climate change. The three-dimensional tapestry creates a lichen effect and black textured surfaces evoke volcanic rock. The vibrancy diminishes down the sculpture until it pools on the floor as a symbol of extinction. Like all of Marta's work, it invites viewers to interact and engage with both the object and topic. 'On one hand, I want people to be curious, surprised, have fun and have an exploratory mindset. On the other hand, I want them to think about the themes and narratives the works are focusing on.'

51

Left, clockwise from top: *Elementary Abacus; Creatures of Light; Prima Familia and the Cossack and Queen.* Photographer: Jonathon Griggs

HELLO SUNSHINE

~~~

Designer: Office S&M
Project name: Graphic House
Location: London, United Kingdom

Photographer: French+Tye

This Edwardian house in London wasn't in great shape when the owners bought it, so they engaged Office S&M to fix and freshen it up to create a generous and connected kitchen and honour the history of the house. As graphic designers, they also wanted to incorporate geometric shapes and playful colour as a way to inform movement through the house, like wayfinding, and to influence the atmosphere and mood of the space. 'The new design draws upon the client's belief in the power of graphics and love of art deco forms, with distinct shapes used to connect spaces and bright colours to enhance every room,' says architect and designer Catrina Stewart, co-founder of Office S&M.

The design team selected specific colours to define key features and help tell a story about the house and its history. These colours are inspired by the family of four's love of the outdoors, as well as the colours in the neighbouring park and back garden, and they tie all the spaces together. Green indicates newly built elements on the ground floor, while bright yellow frames the new windows and doors. The timber stair is fresh blue and existing walls have been restored with the pink plaster left bare.

As you enter, minty green walls line the hallway, with doors opening to the powder room and cupboards that are painted vivid peach – an unexpected bolt of colour that spills into the hall when the door is ajar.

Office S&M removed a wall in the kitchen to create a larger space that connects to the back garden and living room and brings in more natural light. Green continues through the joinery, with strong pops of yellow, blue, pink and red defining elements and objects throughout. Yellow, blue and pink are also splattered through the kitchen benchtops, which are made from recycled white milk bottles and melted-down coloured cutlery and plates. 'It's like having the residues of a feast actually make your kitchen table,' Catrina says.

The clients loved the curved edges in the existing brick walls and glorious art deco fireplace and wanted them continued through the house. The kitchen island benchtop is rounded at each end, and the curved wall enveloping the powder room softens the transition and flow between the kitchen and dining area, and has a gradient of colour as the light hits it.

Circular shapes also feature throughout. A round window in the kitchen frames a view of the garden and acts as a time marker, like the oculus in the dome of the Pantheon in Rome. 'The circle of sunlight will track across the space, recording the passing of time and the seasons. When the circle first appears, it announces the beginning of spring, and its disappearance marks the start of winter,' Catrina explains.

Painted and mirrored circles on the entry wall create a graphic composition that shifts with movement through the space. Painted shapes continuing up the stairwell wall overlap between the different levels, creating connection and informing direction. A large circle rises from the ground floor to the first floor, and a giant stepped shape leads onward and upward from the first flight of stairs. On the top floor, a reflective yellow circle bounces sunlight from the skylight down the stairwell.

Office S&M freshened up the bedrooms on the first and second floors and designed a new, larger family bathroom. Curves and graphic shapes play out in the amoeba-shaped mirror and the rounded shower wall, with yellow grout highlighting the grid of the white wall tiles and unifying the room.

Throughout Graphic House, the plays of colour, light and geometry encourage exploration and create a sense of playfulness that embeds the clients' personality and interests in the design of their house.

54

Previous page: The kitchen opens to the back garden, and sunlight tracks across the space through the round window.

Right: A curved wall softens the transition between the dining area and kitchen.
Following page: The kitchen benchtops are made from recycled white milk bottles and melted-down coloured plastic plates and utensils.

Above, clockwise: Overlapping painted and mirrored circles create a graphic composition at the entry; The existing living room has herringbone timber floors and a glorious art deco fireplace; Bright yellow frames add a pop of colour to the bedroom.

Right: The powder room is painted in bright Dulux Bongo Jazz, which spills out into the minty green hallway.
Following page: Yellow grout highlights the grid of white tiles that wrap around the shower wall in the bathroom.

'This house had to fulfil a series
of practical functions to improve the
lives of the family that occupy it,
but that doesn't mean we can't also
merge these with bold aesthetic choices.
Graphic House demonstrates that
materials, colour, light and
space can transform how we live
in an entirely positive way.'

Catrina Stewart, co-founder
and designer, Office S&M

Office S&M

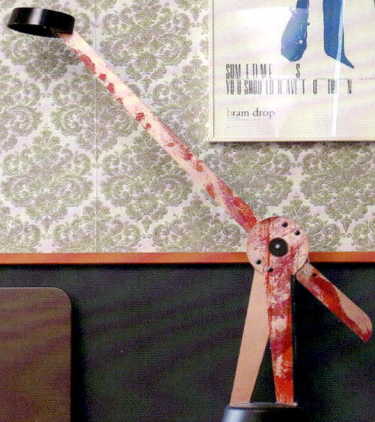

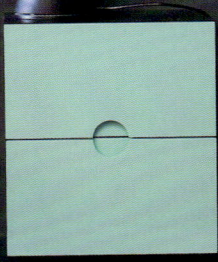

SERIOUS FUN

~~~

Architect/designer: Marcante Testa
Collaborator: Giada Mazzero
Project name: Explosive Compound
Location: Cavallermaggiore, Italy

Photographer: Carola Ripamonti

Built in the 1860s and located in Cavallermaggiore in north-west Italy, Explosive Compound has a storied history. It was originally home to Ascanio Sobrero, who discovered nitroglycerine, which Alfred Nobel used to develop dynamite. It was then home to Ascanio's twin brother, followed by a countess and her husband. The countess sold part of the property to the grandparents of the current owners – another set of twin brothers who grew up in the house. Their parents renovated it in the 1970s, and when one brother, Enrico, decided to move back in, he engaged Marcante Testa to freshen up the dark, drab interior without losing the *memoria storica* (historical memory). 'We had been looking for a project like this. One that had nothing to do with restoration in the historic sense of the word, but everything to do with the lives and memories of the people who had inhabited the space,' says architect and designer Adelaide Testa.

Marcante Testa treated the original architecture and the 1970s renovation equally, choosing to ignore artificial hierarchies of 'high culture' and 'mass culture' and honour the brothers' childhood memories. 'Our desire was to transform it while leaving it unaltered. To create a contemporary interior that keeps and enhances elements from the past, creating a collection of material and sentimental memories,' says architect and designer Andrea Marcante. The result puts the fun into functional, which is reflective of the studio's tongue-in-cheek approach to design.

A new architectural gate and staircase forms the entry to upstairs. The stacked red-brick base references a rural barn in front of the house and the metal-and-mesh structure was inspired by old chicken coops, recalling the chickens that the countess's husband once raised. The metal and mesh continue through the house as a decorative element and a framing and screening mechanism that binds the layers of history together. The bright orange framework connects rooms, curates views and integrates furniture pieces. It also frames sections of patterned 1970s wallpaper and other vestiges, elevating the status of what might be considered kitsch.

A corridor of green resin flooring connects the entrance, living area, kitchen and bathroom, contrasting with the existing flooring that varies from room to room. The floor tiles in the entrance date from the 1970s, while the terracotta tiles in the living room probably date back to the 1860s. The marble fireplace and wood panelling are also original, with new metal inserts providing shelving, and the television concealed within the curtained *teatrino* (puppet theatre).

In the kitchen, a strip of sunflower tiles brightens the custom wood-veneer cabinetry, and the new handles are perfectly colour matched to the sunflowers. Marcante Testa used a digital colour reader to take the chromatic temperature of the sunflowers and many other decorative details, including the bedside tables, wall paint and bathroom vanity.

Enrico's collection of vintage Italian furniture introduces more layers of history. The dining room is home to a 1970s purple fibreglass table attributed to Alberto Rosselli, Alpha-beta ceiling lamps designed by Luca Nichetto for Hem and a Paesaggi Italiani mirror cabinet manufactured by Edra.

Explosive Compound celebrates both its original form and 1970s renovation with a contemporary layer that unites the old and new elements with respect and wry amusement. All eras of design and history are treated equally, as it is the accumulation of layers and meaning that form the backdrop to the brothers' life and memories.

Previous page: The layering of old and new can be seen in the bedroom, where 1970s wallpaper is framed with orange steel.

Right: The bright orange framework connects rooms, frames views and integrates furniture pieces.

Marcante Testa

66

Above: A loggia at the top of the stairs provides a place to sit outdoors and the entry to the house.

Right: The new stair has a stacked red-brick base that references rural barns, and a metal-and-mesh structure inspired by old chicken coops. Following page: The living room with original wood panelling and marble fireplace. A television is concealed in the curtained *teatrino*.

Marcante Testa

'We enjoy walking the line between the serious and amusing. Not all locations transmit a sense of fun, but here it was fundamental.'

Adelaide Testa, co-founder
and architect, Marcante Testa

Previous page: The dining room with a 1970s table attributed to Alberto Rosselli, and Alphabeta ceiling lamps designed by Luca Nichetto for Hem.

Above, left to right: Yellow cabinetry handles have been colour matched to the sunflower pattern in the kitchen; A 1970s applique wall lamp is framed with a panel of orange metal in the entry foyer.
Right: The orange framework morphs into a counter at the entry to the kitchen.

Serious Fun

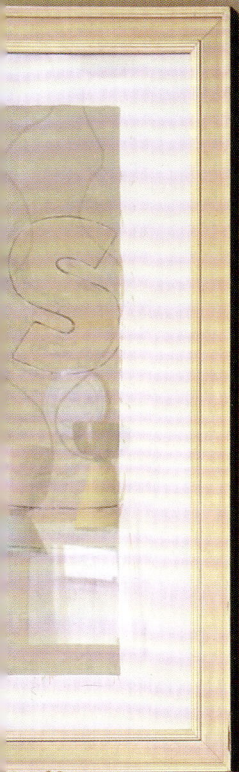

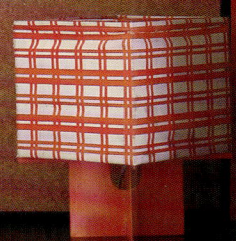

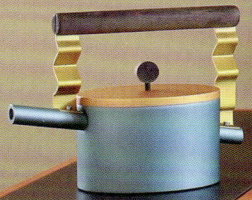

CONCRETE CONNECTIONS

~~~

Architect: Studio Ben Allen
Project name: The House Recast
Location: London, United Kingdom

Photographer: French+Tye
Interior concrete: Concreations
Structural and exterior concrete: Cornish Concrete Products

The owners of The House Recast, a retired couple, had lived in their Victorian-era home in London for about forty years. Frustrated with the rear layout of the house, they approached Studio Ben Allen to design a two-storey extension with a new kitchen and two bathrooms, and encouraged the studio to use the project as a testbed for ideas. 'They were open in terms of colours and materials, and we saw an opportunity to do something quite exciting. We wanted to make concrete an emphasis and take it to a new level,' says architect Ben Allen. Using pigmented, patterned concrete as both the structure and finish infused colour and ornament into the architecture and experience of the terrace.

Victorian houses are typically disconnected from their back gardens, and many have been renovated by adding a boxy volume with a glass wall to improve space, light and aspect. Studio Ben Allen took a different approach, designing an addition that offers more intriguing volumes, spaces and connections.

The use of concrete was inspired by the surrounding Victorian architecture, in which the decorative brickwork is also a structural material. The colours were drawn from High Victorian Gothic architecture and from Orientalism, which fed into the Victorian colour schemes. 'Exoticism in this strain of Victorian architecture was more radical and used colour and pattern in a more adventurous way,' Ben explains. The chosen colours have natural undertones, with pigments from mineral extracts, and elements coloured by use. Green identifies the primary structure, seen in the internal and external columns and beams, while terracotta is used for the secondary structure and finishes, except for the green bathroom.

The intersection of volumes, forms and colours through the kitchen makes for a dynamic composition and spatial experience, and brings light in from multiple directions. The kitchen is a split-level lower than the front room, and arched and rectangular openings connect the two spaces and allow views. Ben says, 'I love putting a hole in a wall to create more elaborate spatial sequences and different connections. No disrespect to the building, but these terraces were made in thousands.'

When you step down into the kitchen, a double-height void rises alongside the curved mezzanine above you. An arched opening above the structural green beam is the start of a vaulted louvred ceiling, mimicking the shape of an arched window in the end brick wall. Viewed from different perspectives, these shapes, volumes and openings create interesting viewpoints, lighting effects and visual connections through the house.

The first-floor bathroom is also concrete, and its lower half and amenities are pigmented in green. The vaulted louvred ceiling diffuses light into the Turkish bath–like chamber, designed as a place to spend time and relax in. The rear facade can be seen through the bathroom window, its scalloped pattern repeated in the green external columns and beams and the bright blue CNC-cut MDF of the mezzanine banister. 'We used a kit of parts to create a graphic connection from one part of the house to another.'

Colour and pattern are vital to The House Recast. They are baked into the architecture, rather than being a decorative afterthought. It's an approach that recalls Memphis – colour is conceived with the design, forming an integral part of the volume and structure. The result is a captivating series of spaces that flow, overlap and intersect, enlivening the experience and connections through the house.

76

Studio Ben Allen

Studio Ben Allen

Previous page: Volumes, forms and colours intersect in the kitchen to create a vibrant and dynamic composition.

Above: Light enters the kitchen through the vaulted ceiling, mezzanine void and the glass doors to the garden
Right: A wall hatch connects the living room and kitchen for serving tea.

Concrete Connections

'People see postmodernism as bright colours and audacious use of classical shapes. But underneath, I think the idea is about reengaging with a more playful and less serious way of making architecture. To do it with enjoyment and make it fun or sightly cheeky.'

Ben Allen, founder
and architect, Studio Ben Allen

Studio Ben Allen

84

Previous page: The mezzanine banister is bright blue CNC-cut MDF with a scalloped pattern that echoes the concrete on the rear facade.
Above, left to right: The bathroom is formed with green concrete, pigmented with mineral extracts; Light filters through the vaulted louvred ceiling.

Right: Arched openings and windows provide views from the mezzanine level to outside.

84

Concrete Connections

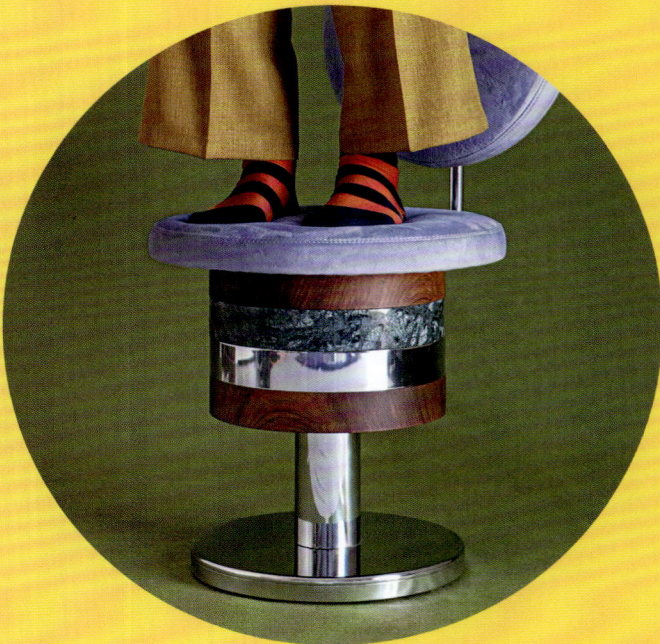

Designer Profile

CHAIRS THAT SPARK JOY

~~~

Designer: Mas Creations
Location: Valencia, Spain

Designers Ana Hernández and Christophe Penasse established Mas Creations to experiment with materials, colours and forms and create furniture and accessories that bring joy to people's day. 'When somebody sees one of our designs for the first time, we want them to be caught by the unexpected, fall in love with it and find the joyful and positive energy,' says Christophe.

Mas Creations evolved out of Ana and Christophe's interior design studio, Masquespacio, which gives life to hospitality and retail spaces with blockbuster colours, eye-catching patterns and bespoke furniture, all driven by strong narrative themes. 'We search for the wow factor in each project, creating an interior that evokes emotions through its detail and that makes visitors feel special, living a new experience,' says Ana.

That panache and emotiveness continue in their Mas Creations furniture and accessories, which are designed independent of client projects or specific markets, developing from investigations into certain topics and specific materials as well as the simple intention to evoke joy and delight. 'We create a lot of emotion and joyful details, while at the same time we get away from a literal and decorative approach. It's a combination of forms, textures, materials and colours that bring it all together in something that we could call an explosive cocktail, as per Ana's character, influenced by past movements, brought to the future,' says Christophe.

Ana is from Colombia and Christophe is from Belgium, and their work is imbued with both fiery passion and scrupulous methodology. This creative tension presents itself in the playful colours of the serious materials and the imaginative forms of the rigorous structures. The Block Chair stands out for its graphic approach to materials, with the layered cylinder of marble, wood and stainless steel anchoring the base. 'We are in love with materials that have a certain connection point with earth and hereby are more human. We like to contrast materials and colours, as well as challenge unidentified material combinations, creating new textures and forms with them,' says Christophe.

Similarly, the Secrétaire chair rests on stacked semi-circular blocks within the stainless steel frame. Connecting two chairs, like a tête-à-tête, the Secrétaire is a romantic interpretation of the seating traditionally placed in the foyers of ancient buildings.

In giving life to new pieces, Ana and Christophe feel they give life in general. Christophe says, 'The idea behind the design was to represent a person by itself because Ana is always dreaming that furniture and objects are persons in the interior.' This is particularly so for the Too Much Rocking Chair. The round lines and forms express the dynamism of the chair, and the alternating strips of marble create a mesmerising, graphic effect when in motion. When it is still, the chair rests on a marble wedge stopper, showcasing the designers' meticulous attention to detail. Too much? Never!

Left, clockwise: Too Much Rocking Chair; Secrétaire; Block Chair.
Photographer: Masquespacio

SUPER GRAPHIC

~~~

Designer: Studio Sam Buckley
Project name: Merchiston Crescent
Location: Edinburgh, United Kingdom

Photographer: Alix McIntosh

'Experimentation is key,' says architectural technologist and interior designer Sam Buckley, founder of Studio Sam Buckley. He experimented with bold colour and graphic shapes on a super-sized scale in this Victorian-era apartment in Edinburgh, saturating the interior to create a technicolour immersion and sparing no surface. This approach harks back to the Supergraphics movement of the 1960s and 1970s, which saw buildings and spaces painted with colourful ribbons, swirls and geometric forms, creating a sense of movement and optical illusion. 'It's about graphic design for walls, doors and ceilings and celebrates bold design on an outrageous scale,' Sam says.

The client – a game designer – engaged Sam to design a home that would provoke visitors to say 'Wow!' At the time, Sam was developing a carpet collection for cc-tapis, exploring geometric compositions with interlocking and overlapping circles and semicircles dictated by a set of rules and grid he established. He designed a bespoke rug based on this series to ground the large living space of the apartment, and adapted the arrangement to a smaller scale for the custom enamel push plates on the doors.

Sam also became interested in the Supergraphics movement at this time, and he applied his interest in colour and geometry to the walls to create an immersive environment. 'As a rebellion against the white box, I explored the use and application of colour and how it can affect the mood of a space. A lot of people think it would be distracting to sit in a space like this, but actually it's quite calming.'

The walls and ceiling become an active part of the interior, with vibrant colour and geometric shapes, sometimes accounting for the architectural mouldings and sometimes ignoring them. The placement and layering of the circles, ovals, arches and triangles plays with perspective, creating a sense of movement and illusion, depending on where you are in the room. An oval stretches through the windows, a row of small triangles spike from the side of the bookcase and across the doorway, and circles and arches radiate around the rose-tinted mirror.

The colour palette originated from the green, blue, turquoise and yellow velvet of the sofa, which Sam balanced with warmer colours of pink, deep coral and maroon. The colours and shapes are continued through furnishings and lighting to create harmony and unity. The golden yellow pendant light pairs a circle and semicircle, and the side tables combine a multitude of shapes. The plasterwork ceiling rose, designed in collaboration with Chalk Plaster, is also part of the same geometric language, conceived in three-dimensional form. The bedroom is more subtle with a relatively neutral paint palette on the walls, yet still in keeping with the bold, graphic style.

If you imagine the apartment without the painted walls and ceiling, it becomes a rather pared-back space, which is why Sam describes his approach as chromatic minimalism. 'I like minimalism in many ways for the lack of fussy design, but I get tired of it in shades of beige, black and white. I feel more drawn to chromatic minimalism, but every job is totally unique, and I like to experiment too much to be tied down to a single style,' he explains.

Previous page: A Vipp floor lamp and Shuffle side table by &Tradition next to a bright orange chair.

Right and following page: The living room is an immersive environment with coloured geometric shapes across the walls, rug and furniture. The bespoke cc-tapis rug is part of an ongoing series that Sam is designing called DiscoRectangle.

Studio Sam Buckley

Studio Sam Buckley

'Interiors are such individual and personal spaces that to try and establish a norm is to whitewash an artistic endeavour. That, in my opinion, is a disservice to the industry.'

Sam Buckley, designer,
Studio Sam Buckley

Above: The vibrant colour and geometric shapes painted across the walls and ceiling sometimes account for the architectural mouldings and sometimes ignore them.

Right and previous page: Sam adapted the geometric arrangement of the rug for the custom enamel push plates on the doors. Each push plate has a different arrangement.

Studio Sam Buckley

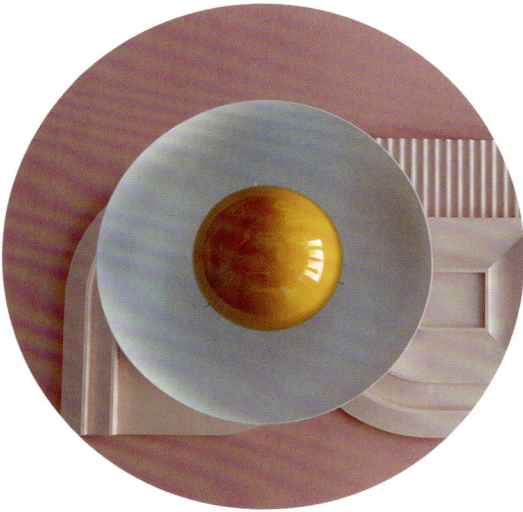

Left: The bedroom has geometric shapes painted on the wall in a more subtle and subdued palette.

Above, top left: A Verner Panton pendant light hangs from the ceiling rose;
Bottom left and right: The wall and fireplace mantle are painted blue at one end and maroon at the other, and decorative objects have curved, striped forms.

Studio Sam Buckley

MICRO-COSMIC

~~~

Designer: Point Supreme Architects
Project name: Nadja
Location: Athens, Greece

Photographers: Yannis Drakoulidis, Efi Gousi
Construction: KN Group

This Athens apartment, designed by Point Supreme Architects, is a microcosm for the owners, yet it has a vastness that feels greater than its size. 'As soon as you enter you are pleasantly lost in an open space whose borders you don't see or feel. It is a house far from familiar, namely a box with rooms where the limits are clear and there are standard rules for how functions work,' says architect Konstantinos Pantazis.

The apartment is home to a family of five. The owner-builders engaged Point Supreme to combine two separate apartments, one on each floor, and to create spaces that facilitated their social and active lifestyle. The clients were also involved in the colour and material selection, working with the design team to create a playful home that reflects their personalities and has symbolic references to Greece's nautical heritage and architecture. 'When different colours, patterns and symbols are at play, the result can be an interesting collision,' says Konstantinos.

A new staircase in the middle of the floor plan unites the apartments. The bedrooms are located on the upper floor, and the kitchen, living and dining spaces are on the lower floor. Downstairs is an expansive, connected space that fosters spontaneity and improvisation. A sea of shimmering blue floor tiles creates a marine-like ambience, with large pieces of furniture acting like floating islands, anchoring the family's communal activities. Strips of triangular black-and-white tiles indicate thresholds and points of transition, inspired by the ferries that travel between the Greek islands. 'These patterns mark the steps or different plateaus, so they subconsciously create the feeling of being on a boat platform.'

At the heart of this room is a multifaceted, playful construction that serves as a focal and circulatory point within the open space. It cleverly combines the staircase, living room and kitchen cupboards, a benchtop, a built-in planter and a blackboard. With an open triangle beneath the stair and benchtop, and glass panes and windows above the stair, the kids and the cat use this dynamic piece of mini-architecture like a jungle gym, moving through and around it in unconventional ways.

The bright yellow staircase takes you upstairs, past the pink sun, where there is an earthier palette and atmosphere. Each of the children's bedrooms has its own colour and character, and subtly combines a social area and a sleeping zone, like a room within a room. One bed is surrounded by dark blue walls and has planets overhead to evoke outer space, while another is set within an arched yellow alcove inspired by a Greek island tradition. The third bedroom has a cartoon mural with a pirate boat, and a timber platform on the floor opens up so a sheet can be hoisted and the kids can set sail.

The design – and in some cases the non-design – of this apartment encourages possibility and spontaneity, enriching the family's life. With this flexibility, freedom and atmosphere, the family have become closely attached to their home. 'They used to travel a lot, but after they moved in, they didn't want to travel so much because they missed being in the space. It became like a new member of the family,' says Konstantinos.

Previous page: A small architectural construction combines staircase, living room and kitchen cupboards, a benchtop, a built-in planter and a blackboard.

Right: The downstairs living area is a large open space with a floor of glistening blue tiles and large pieces of timber furniture.
Following page: A strip of triangular black-and-white tiles marks the transition between spaces.

'We make sure the space leaves freedom for improvisation and liberty in how people use it. It's like jokes. There's something more interesting when you have to fill them in, create them in your mind.'

Konstantinos Pantazis, co-founder
and architect, Point Supreme Architects

Point Supreme Architects

Previous page: The downstairs bathroom has a pebbled floor. A timber-dowel partition physically delineates the entry from the kitchen and dining area.

Above: A painted pink sun rises on the wall upstairs alongside the bright yellow stair.

Above: Each of the three children's bedrooms is designed as a room within a room, combining a social area and a sleeping zone.

CHEQUERED PAST

~~~

Architect/designer: Fieldwork
Project name: Rose Street Residence
Location: Melbourne, Australia

Photographer: Tom Ross
Landscaper: Mud Office

Rose Street Residence, in the back streets of Melbourne, has had a colourful past. The Victorian-era terrace was an abandoned brothel when Paul Ghaie, co-founder of neighbourhood wine stores Blackhearts & Sparrows, and Lucy Wallace, a hospitality professional, purchased it. They engaged Fieldwork to transform the terrace into a contemporary home. Fieldwork embraced the disorder and decadence of the former brothel's interior to honour the building's vivid history.

The terrace had seven bedrooms, seven bathrooms and seven 'vibes' – a different mood in each room. Decked out with vermillion and pink walls, yellow velvet curtains, classical detailing, gold Roman columns, plus neon signs and mirrored ceilings, the interior was lurid and gaudy, the trickle-down result of postmodernism. 'It was fascinating and confronting,' says architect Quino Holland. 'Over time we realised that someone had thought carefully about the spaces, design and colours. The initial instinct was to wipe it all away, but then we thought let's have a dialogue with history and extract some positives from the chequered past.'

The existing interior and the open-mindedness and personality of the clients inspired Fieldwork's approach to overlay references to the brothel throughout the house. Clashing, garish colours and unexpected material combinations create contrasting and different atmospheres in every room, while the repetition of colour, light, form and the overall eclecticism ties them together. 'At first you think the colours and materials don't work, but we got to like them and embraced it,' Quino says. He describes the result as Apollo and Dionysus: Apollo being the god of light, reason, harmony and balance, and Dionysus the god of wine, revelry, passion, emotion and instinct.

The front rooms of the terrace have been retained and a new extension added to the rear. The lounge, kitchen and dining spaces are downstairs, and there is a bedroom and bathroom on both levels. Across the landscaped courtyard is a two-storey self-contained apartment, with a single multipurpose space downstairs and two bedrooms, each with spas, upstairs.

Fieldwork created a cinema-like space in the front lounge room to cater for Paul and Lucy's love of music and films. The original floorboards remain, and crushed velvet curtains can be drawn to enclose the room.

The flooring changes to pink-flecked granite in the kitchen, which is the centrepiece of the house for cooking and entertaining. Timber veneer cabinetry is warm and luxe, and the raw brass benchtop will become patinaed with time and use. Brass accents such as the half-moon handles and inset floor trim reference the gaudy gold-painted architraves and cornices of the brothel.

The dining booth is an unabashed combination of fairy floss–pink with olive-green leather and velvet, while gold curtains provide a backdrop to the living room. Coloured film on the high windows is a take on traditional lead glass windows. If you peek behind the gold curtain, you see that the courtyard is illuminated with a red light and a neon pink 'Exquisite Ladies' sign, both a literal nod to the brothel. In the self-contained apartment, pink LED leads up the staircase and around the perimeter of the rooms, bathing the textured white walls with a hue that matches the peach carpets.

Back in the main house, the black-and-white mosaic tiling and blue joinery in the downstairs bathroom are inspired by the 'grim' bathroom that formerly occupied the space. Upstairs, the bathroom shifts in atmosphere and aesthetic depending on the time of day, sunlight and weather. At night, it is white with shiny bottle-green tiles. By day, a pink film on the skylight bathes it in a rose-coloured glow.

Rose Street Residence is a cohesive fusing of a Victorian terrace and modern architecture, layered with references that pay homage to the chaotic and colourful character of the brothel. 'The Dionysian spirit is alive and well,' Quino says.

Previous page: A pink film on the skylight in the bathroom bathes the white walls in a rose-coloured glow.

Right: The pink and green dining banquette is by Jason Blake, maker at I Am Not Mason. The custom table is crafted by Chris Scott.
Following page: A sliver of garden down the side of the house brings in light and landscaped views to the kitchen, dining and living areas.

112

115

Above, left to right: The raw brass benchtop will patina over time;
The custom shelving units have a pink metal frame with inlays of granite.
Right: Curved corners on the kitchen island create more circulation
space in a narrow room.

Following page: The back of the house has been rebuilt using bricks
from what was demolished. The neon pink 'Exquisite Ladies' sign is a literal
nod to the former brothel.

Chequered Past

'The typical instinct with small houses is to do a single material palette and idea, whereas we took a different approach. We wanted to create contrasting moods and different atmospheres in each of the spaces.'

Quino Holland,
director and architect, Fieldwork

FUN FAIR

~~~

Designer: Studio Job
Project name: Rolf's Apartment
Location: Amsterdam, Netherlands

Photographer: Kasia Gatkowska
Stylist: Barbara Berends

Fasten your seatbelts for a phantasmagorical ride through Rolf's Apartment. Drawing on childhood memories of the Dutch theme park Efteling, designer and artist Job Smeets created a fantastical world for long-time friend and creative collaborator Rolf Snoeren, one half of the avant-garde fashion brand Viktor&Rolf. 'Rolf is the perfect client when it comes to freedom and creation. We have worked together many times and the result is always amazing,' says the founder of Studio Job, who has thrown the maxim 'form follows function' to the wayside.

Rolf and his husband, Brandon O'Dell, gave Job carte blanche for their apartment, which spans the top floor of a traditional canal house. 'The apartment layout is classical, but the visualisation is postmodern and liberal because I have played with expression, scale and unusual materials,' Job says. The subversive design is rich in irony and imagination with mock-castle materials and cartoonish effects. 'All the things we do are very present and they have an impact on your vision. Although it's so powerful and confronting, the atmosphere is very balanced, pleasant and relaxed.'

The plasticky front door, made from shiny brown resin with a three-dimensional textured woodgrain, sets the tone for the apartment and opens to the entrance, which is wrapped with red-and-white candy cane stripes. The carnival vibes peak in the living room, where the wall cabinet is sure to put a smile on your dial. Flames roar in the open mouth of the bronze fireplace, a giant robot face with sparkling eyes clenches its teeth in a grin, a penis-shaped door leads to the library and funfair lights frame the bar cabinet. All this is set on a background of 'crazy paving' wallpaper, which culminates in the staircase that leads to the red heart-shaped rooftop terrace, as if ascending to a castle's turret.

The faux materials continue in the bedroom, sitting room and office. 'Brick' and 'woodgrain' wallpaper bring the look and feel of conventional outside materials inside, playing with perception and visual effect. It's the same in the kitchen, where the joinery and rangehood are covered with a three-dimensional red brick that mimics the real red-brick wall of the terrace.

The pink wall, punctured with deep recessed windows, provides a cotton candy contrast alongside the kitchen and hallway, while the powder room is saturated in yellow and the bathroom in salmon. Here, the custom ceiling light is like cracked glass, ringed with carnival lights, and the mirror reflects the lush rose-adorned windows in the sitting room.

As a conceptual and sculptural artist and designer, Job produces art pieces that elevate popular images, symbols and motifs into objects of desire. In Rolf's Apartment, this includes the bronze fireplace and rock cauldron seat in the living room, as well as the bronze turtles supporting the bed and rose-painted dining table. The regal button-tufted daybed is the perfect spot for gazing across Amsterdam's rooftops, while the pigeon table, originally created for a client whose father is a pigeon fancier, brings out the beauty of the ubiquitous bird.

The apartment was completed in March 2020, right before Amsterdam went into lockdown, and it brought Rolf and Brandon happiness during the pandemic. 'Rolf says how much he loves to be there. It's like living in an experience, in a capsule,' says Job.

Previous page: Brick and Rosewood wallpaper play with perception and visual effect in the bedroom and lounge. The tiny bronze chair is by Studio Job.

Right: 'Flat Stones' crazy paving wallpaper provides a lively backdrop to Studio Job's Rose Table and customised Fledermaus dining chairs by Josef Hoffmann. The stairs lead to the rooftop terrace.

Studio Job

124

Studio Job

Previous page: Wall cabinetry animates the living area, which features many Studio Job designs, including the bronze fireplace, rock cauldron seat and pigeon table.

Above, left to right: The plasticky front door is made is from shiny brown resin with a three-dimensional textured woodgrain; The custom 'brick' kitchen features decorative objects and lamps by Studio Job.

Above: In the lounge outside the bedroom, a Marzio Cecchi Balestra lounge chair faces the windows treated with a 'Wild Roses' design.

Following page: The cabinetry also integrates a bar, framed with yellow trim and funfair lights.

'I have been connected with many different styles throughout the years: Postmodernism, Gothic, Gothic Pop, Neo Baroque, Renaissance, Symbolism. If you put it all together, it is all some kind of postmodernism.'

Job Smeets, artist,
designer and founder, Studio Job

Studio Job

Above, clockwise: A tiny bronze chair by Studio Job sits in front of the bed; Studio Job's Frying Pan mirror for Ghidini 1961 hangs in the bathroom, and porcelain Axe in the alcove of the pink wall; The salmon-coloured bathroom has a ceiling light ringed with carnival lights.

Right: A velvet daybed offers prime position for views of Amsterdam. It is accompanied by a David Altmejd sculpture, and Studio Job's bronze table and Tour Eiffel lamp.

SWEET SPOT

~~~

Designer: 2LG Studio
Project name: The Design House
Location: London, United Kingdom

Photographer: Megan Taylor

Jordan Cluroe and Russell Whitehead, the interior design duo behind 2LG Studio, transformed their rundown 1870s Victorian house in London into a creative and expressive home and workspace called The Design House that hits the sweet spot. Achieving an aesthetic they call 'joyful minimalism', Jordan and Russell honoured the heritage of the house, layered it with jubilant colour and modern materials, and infused the home with personal memories and references. 'We wanted to achieve a space that did not adhere to any rules, and that expressed who we are,' Russell says.

The house needed fixing up and modernising when the couple bought it, but they instantly connected with its 'beautiful bones' and 'wonderful soul' as well as its remnants of colours: pastel-pink walls in the entrance hallway and deep-green carpet on the stairs.

Challenging the divisive conventions of colour, pink takes pride of place through the home. 'It feels like a queer statement in very basic terms, as we were always told as men we were not allowed to wear pink or live in pink spaces. We don't like boundaries or closed doors. We tend to drive straight through them,' says Jordan. In the entrance hall, the pink hand-drawn wallpaper, designed with felt-tip pens, is a playful contrast to the grandeur of the deep blue carpet, which is based on an 1870s design in the archives of the carpet manufacturer Brintons.

The front sitting room is light and airy with soft pops of colour, sculptural forms and reinstated wall panelling and period details. Splashes of colour intensify in the kitchen and dining area, where the doorways are framed with squiggles of fairy floss–pink, inspired by Ettore Sottsass's Ultrafragola mirror. 'It's lipstick for doors, and breaks the convention of period architraves,' Russell says. Pale pink prevails through the kitchen, where two tall arched cupboards maintain a minimalist aesthetic and the curves bring a light-hearted spirit to the design, breaking strong lines and hard edges.

These forms are repeated in the cupboards in the dining room, where the juxtaposition of bright green for the wall and table enlivens the look and feel. 'When we designed the Jesmonite table with Olivia Aspinall in 2017, the 1970s crazy paving style of the large chunks felt boundary pushing and the marbling of the colours was an experiment that we ended up falling in love with. It's called Stanley. After Kubrick. We love his work and design aesthetic, and pop culture often infuses our designs,' says Russell.

Creative collaboration was key to this design. The pair reached out to makers, designers, friends and brands to create bespoke and meaningful pieces with them. This includes the sofa, chairs, beds, joinery and capsule strip lights, as well as the wallpaper in the entrance and the powder room, nicknamed the Wonder Closet (WC). The powder room wallpaper is handprinted with metallic details based on a tiny ditsy floral wallpaper that was uncovered beneath layers of paint and old wall coverings. 'It's like a little jewel box when you are in there. It makes for a fun conversation with dinner guests,' Jordan says.

Upstairs, there are two bedrooms, a dressing room and a writing room overlooking the garden. Bright blues, pretty pinks and lavenders continue on the walls, joinery and ceiling, with lime green and vivid yellow thrown in for good measure. They used bright blue for its energising qualities, upholstering the curves of the bedhead in blue velvet and painting the ceiling of their writing room in Yves Klein blue.

Filled with a candy-coloured assortment of playful shapes, saturated surfaces and collaborative endeavours, Jordan and Russell's home is a total delight. It embodies their vision, expresses their personalities and celebrates creative freedom. 'When people come to our house, they immediately look around wide-eyed, like children in a sweet shop, and that is wonderful to see,' says Russell.

134

Previous page: Wooden mouldings have been added to the front living room to mimic the panelling that may have been there originally.

Right: The pink hand-drawn wallpaper connects circulation spaces through the house. The carpet is based on a design from the 1870s, when the house was built.

2LG Studio

2LG Studio

Previous page: The Tilda sofa and armchairs, designed by 2LG Studio with Love Your Home, have curved corners for extra comfort when lying down.

Above: Jordan and Russell eat, host friends, make art, design and present to clients in the dining room they designed with Olivia Aspinall.

Above: 2LG Studio designed the kitchen and dining room cabinetry
in collaboration with John Lewis of Hungerford.

'The Memphis design movement enchanted us at an early stage in our design careers as it connected with our queerness. It felt aligned with how we feel as queer designers, with a focus on expression and exuberance and openness. Stability and sensibleness are born out of fear and we try to be as fearless as we can. Disruption is an important thing.'

Jordan Cluroe and Russell Whitehead,
founders and designers, Studio 2LG

2LG Studio

Previous page: Strip capsule lights are coloured pink and green to match the dining room and kitchen.
Left: The curves and colour palette continue in this bright pink dresser and chair.

Above, left to right: A wavy edge adds a playful detail to the wardrobe joinery, along with the bright yellow fabric that is reflected in the glass panels; The ceiling of the writing room is painted Yves Klein blue for an energising atmosphere.

2LG Studio

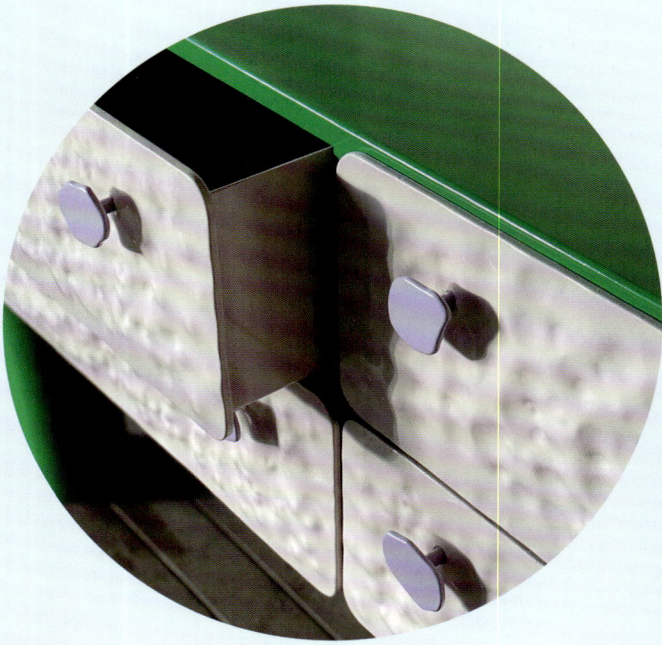

BROTHERS AT PLAY

~~~

Designer: Fearon
Location: Gold Coast, Australia

It was a slow and unexpected shift into designing and making furniture for brothers Jack and Mark Fearon, who trained and worked in plumbing and boilermaking. But their expert fabrication skills and love of colour has seen them produce imaginative pieces that are as sophisticated as they are childlike.

The Queensland-based brothers were making large water trucks when they decided to open their own fabrication business and create custom steel structures, such as doors, staircases and gates. One thing led to another, and they conceived the idea for the Chub stool using offcuts from the water trucks. The versatile piece can be used as a stool, step, bedside table, bookshelf or even a shower stand. The versatility is not only in its multiple uses, but also in its longevity, which is core to Fearon's design philosophy. 'If you buy something from us, we want it to be loved and used in your home forever. It might mean you buy a Chub to use as a stool in your share house, then you take it with you when you move into your own space, then it goes into your kid's room to store books on and then it ends up in their house when they move out,' says Jack.

The most distinctive aspects of the stool are its full-figured legs and the seamless folds that resemble the hip crease of a human body. Welded with care and precision, the aluminium is fashioned to look formed, like ceramics,

and exudes a human touch. 'Even though aluminium is a cold product, we want our products to have a really warm feel to them, and adding colour helps with that,' Jack says. The array of fresh, neutral and bold colours also adds to the warmth and playfulness of the piece.

Speaking of playfulness, Jack and Mark designed the Socks and Undies dresser with Jack's then four-month-old daughter in mind. The structure retains the chubby legs, the dimpled front of the drawers ripple with light and shadow, and the irregular handles are inspired by candy.

The idea for their ten-seater dining table came when Jack's wife was pregnant and the couple were eating a lot of pancakes for dinner. While the inspiration might not have been literal, it was subconscious, and Jack fondly named the table Pancakes for Dinner. 'Once we had finished the table, that's all I could think about when I looked at it,' he says. The tabletop has wide scalloped edges and the base has layers of cloud-like shapes in different colours.

As well as being skilfully designed and exceptionally well crafted, there is a naivety and innocence in Fearon's pieces that reflects the brothers' imagination and elevates the form of these objects far beyond their basic functions. 'Art can bleed into objects and I want our pieces to provoke a sense of fun in people's homes while also being durable, well-made and versatile in their uses,' Jack says.

145

Left, clockwise: Socks and Undies dresser; Pancakes for Dinner table; Chub stool. Photographers: Jack Fearon and Jordan Malane

DAVID SMITH

AESTHETICS OF HAPPINESS

Designer: Ghislaine Viñas
Architect: Chet Architecture
Project name: LA Residence
Location: Los Angeles, United States

Photographer: Garrett Rowland
Art consultant: Paige West

Interior designer Ghislaine Viñas is a strong believer in what she terms the 'aesthetics of happiness,' and it abounds in this Los Angeles residence. Ghislaine designed the interior with and for architect Chet Callahan, who shares the home with his husband, Jacinto, and their two sons. It's the second house Ghislaine has designed with Chet, and this time they dialled it up a notch. Exuding happiness and whimsy, the interior is a reflection and representation of the residents and a sure sign Ghislaine and Chet enjoy collaborating.

The house, originally known as Cummings Estate, was the first estate in Los Feliz, built around the turn of the 20th century. Chet describes the style as 'quasi-Craftsman with elements borrowed from Spanish and other architectural styles.' He extended the house with a glass and terrazzo-clad addition accommodating a new kitchen, terrace and carport, and making a clear distinction between the old and new. This juxtaposition of traditional and modern continues throughout the interior, with clean minimalist architectural elements inserted among the restored historical features and complementing and contrasting with the wood panelling.

As part of Ghislaine's design process, she asks clients what happiness looks and feels like to them. 'The aesthetics of happiness is about capturing what makes someone happy and what makes them feel good,' Ghislaine explains. 'Chet and Jacinto wanted the house to feel like a fictional character had lived in the house from the time it was built, traveling the world for the past 120 years and collecting items from around the globe.' The couple also wanted references to their lives and an art collection that showcases 'identity' and 'representation' for them and their children. These, together with the history of the house, planted the seeds for a narrative approach to the decor, in which every room has a main protagonist that tells a story.

In the entry foyer, the custom-designed rug is detailed with a line drawing of the house and a series of black lines that ascend the grand wooden stairs, evoking the carpets and stair runners in the foyers of traditional hotels. The custom rug in the living room is also detailed with a line drawing, this time an abstraction of Alexander Calder's stabile sculpture at Bank of America Plaza, where Jacinto used to work.

Ghislaine selected furnishings and lighting from different countries and eras to create an eclectic, modern feel. 'I wanted pairings you might not imagine,' she says. The living room has a glam 1970s vibe with a curved leather sofa, two angular armchairs and gold metallic coffee table, while the dining room is enchanting and ethereal, with a pale pink stain applied to the wood panelling, and blush pink for the rug, chairs and terrazzo table. The deep red, tongue-in-cheek powder room features a neon sign reading 'It's a Shit Show' bathing the hand-painted trompe l'oeil wallpaper. Ghislaine also designed custom furniture throughout, many pieces with circular forms and soft curves, like the green table and sideboard in the breakfast room and the pill-shaped cabinet in the bathroom. 'Living with softer, rounder shapes feels good and brings so much joy,' she says.

Chet and Jacinto's art collection is as integral to the aesthetics and narrative of the interior as the furniture and architecture. The couple worked with art consultant Paige West of Mixed Greens to collect pieces by Black, Native American and queer artists that represent their experiences, backgrounds, interests and identities, as well as their children's.

While there is a sense of spontaneity in the design, make no mistake – every element is carefully considered and curated. This home emanates a palpable sense of happiness and joy, with every element playing its part in telling the story of Chet, Jacinto and their children.

Previous page: The family room has a canopy of PET Lamp shades suspended over Jaime Hayon's Multileg table.

Right: The new stair sweeps over the kitchen, where Brett Murray's *Little Bubble* artwork boldly states 'Oprah Says Live Life Deliciously'.

Ghislaine Viñas and Chet Architecture

150

Above: Ghislaine custom designed the rug and stair runner in the entry foyer, which also features a marble console by Joris Poggioli and mirror by Zieta. Right: The entry offers a view into the dining room, with a yellow and pink artwork tying the two colour palettes together.

Following page: A white leather De Sede sofa wraps around a Karl Springer table. Ghislaine upholstered the Utrecht armchairs, designed by Gerrit Rietveld, in a graphic print from Dimorestudio.

Ghislaine Viñas and Chet Architecture

'I design spaces to be positive
so clients walk in and feel good.
I don't think people realise how much
fun it can be to design their home
and make it joyful and unique.'

Ghislaine Viñas,
interior and product designer

Ghislaine Viñas and Chet Architecture

Previous page: Ghislaine designed the table and sideboard in the breakfast room, where two paintings by Derrick Adams hang on the wall. The fibreglass chairs from Modernica were originally designed by Eames in 1948.

Left and above: Artist Adrian Kay Wong painted the mural on the interior walls of the staircase, with the stair treads carpeted bright blue.

Ghislaine Viñas and Chet Architecture

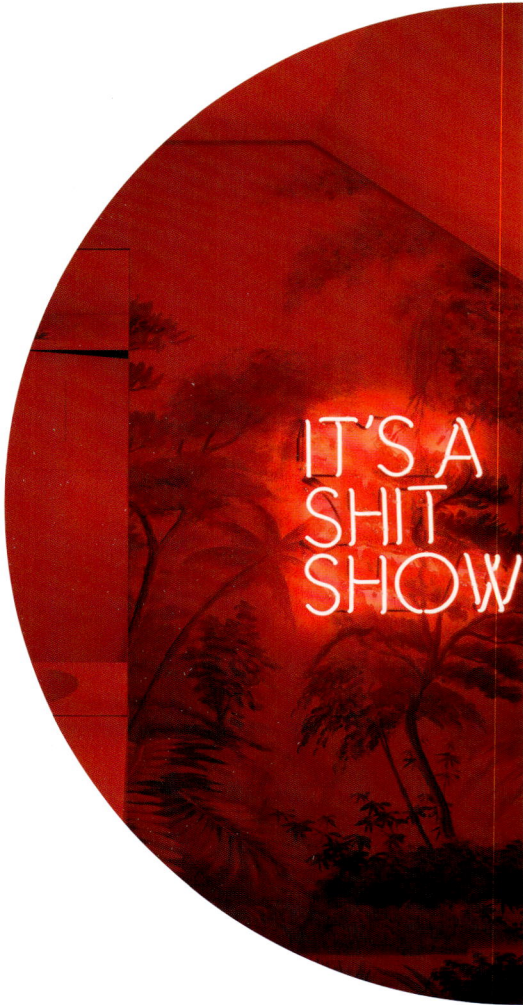

158

Above, left to right: The neon light casts a deep red hue over the powder room; The dining room has a soft pink tinge with a pale pink stain applied to the wood panelling, and the dining chairs by A Rudin are upholstered in blush pink.

Right: The curved design of the bathroom cabinet evokes the shape of a pill.

NO HOLDS BARRED

~~~

Designer: Jassy
Project name: Jassy's House
Location: New Orleans, United States

Photographer: Jacqueline Marque

Jassy didn't hold back on the design of his New Orleans home, painting and crafting rooms and furniture in a bold, cartoonish style that reflects his personal aesthetic and fantasy-filled life. The avid anime fan is a producer and performer in the drag wrestling show *Choke Hole*. His persona is a crazed real estate investor/landlord sporting fashion straight out of the 1980s – think neon orange and pink latex costumes with power-suit shoulder pads and oversized hair to match. That outlandish 1980s style is also alive and well in Jassy's home, with its wild colour, graphic prints, DIY furniture and materials used in imaginative and unconventional ways. 'I love the idea of living in a fantasy. I want to wake up and have a really energetic space that keeps me motivated and inspired,' Jassy says.

The 1920s double-shotgun house is part of New Orleans's architectural vernacular. The two single-storey dwellings share a central wall, with each side having a long, linear floor plan that is just one room wide. Circulation is through each room, rather than a hallway, so moving through Jassy's house is like venturing further into his fantasy land. He designed it room by room and became more comfortable and confident with it over time.

The front room is a dining room and office space with pink and white walls. IKEA bookshelves are framed with wood to create a wall of joinery. A portrait of Michelangelo's *David*, featuring spray-foam hair, takes pride of place in the centre. Jassy made a lot of the furniture himself, using IKEA pieces and vintage and second-hand finds, taking inspiration from designer lighting and popular culture, and bringing his own imaginative ideas to life. His father helped, making the orange chandelier with oversized plastic chains, basing the design on a pendant worth tens of thousands of dollars.

The living room is through a large arched opening. The walls are painted with free-form shapes inspired by the 1974 movie by John Waters, *Female Trouble*. Jassy covered two IKEA coffee tables with square tiles, accentuating the grid pattern, and made the large orange mirror using smaller panes.

Next is a guest bedroom, followed by the bathroom and then Jassy's bedroom. He and his father made the tiled bed from scratch, having seen a 1980s tiled bathtub, and Jassy made the vanity by combining and painting IKEA shelves, vintage pieces and a mirror framed with chain. The full-length mirror with a wavy edge is inspired by the Ultrafragola mirror, as Jassy got more familiar with the style of Memphis and Sottsass during the design. 'I'm a big fan of waves and grids. One's very structural and one's very free-form and natural, and I love how they play off each other,' he says.

Jassy's signature colour, orange, plays a dominant role throughout the house, teamed with blue, aqua, pink and green. The kitchen, at the back of the house, is like an underwater immersion with walls painted green with a wave and blended ombre. The backyard is also painted to create a swimming pool effect. 'I've always wanted a pool, but couldn't afford one, so I painted one like a weird art installation.'

With his no-holds-barred design, Jassy's home makes his imaginative world real and brings his fantasy to life. 'The house gets progressively more untethered from reality. It's like Alice in Wonderland: the deeper into the rabbit hole you go, the more outlandish and trippier it gets,' he says.

162

Previous page: Jassy made the joinery wall using IKEA bookshelves framed with wood trim.

Right: The green cabinets are from Urban Outfitters, and Jassy made the chunky mirror by covering carved-out foam with resin.

Jassy

Jassy

Previous page: The living room walls are painted with colourful free-form shapes. Jassy's dad made the chandelier in the dining room using oversized plastic chains.

Left: Tiles on the coffee tables and mirror create a structural grid pattern that contrasts with the more organic shapes reflected in the mirror.
Above: An acrylic surface has been added to the top of the IKEA cabinet, and a handmade light by Mimi Girouard is on the wall above.

Jassy

168

Above, left to right: Jassy made or altered everything in his bedroom, including painting the orange fireplace and the black-and-white grid, and making the wavy-edged mirror and the tiled bed. A rug by Cold Picnic hangs on the wall as an artwork.

Right: Mirrored panels, blue paint and wood trim have been added to the front of IKEA cabinets. The vanity includes vintage pieces and Moustache's Bold Chair. Following page: Vintage Verner Panton chairs and an inflatable Yomi Eko sofa from Mojow provide fun seating in the backyard.

'I love how outlandish 1980s design is. It was crazy prints and wild colour and everything was oversized and overdone. My performance style and show are very absurd and outlandish and I have always gravitated towards that aesthetic.'

Jassy, designer and maker

Jassy

KALEIDOSCOPIC COLLAGE

Designer: Ayromloo Design
Project name: Mexico City Residence
Location: Mexico City, Mexico

Photographer: Annie Schlechter

The bustling streets of Mexico City provided interior designer Jessica Ayromloo with inspiration for this pied-à-terre. Jessica looked out the window, wandered the streets and explored the local markets to capture the pulse and patchwork of the neighbourhood in its interior. The result is a kaleidoscopic collage of colour, pattern and shapes that visually animate the apartment, creating a sense of movement and illusion and reflecting the energy of the streets outside.

Carlos Rittner, president of CR Creative Services and founder of Artbug Gallery in Los Angeles, engaged Ayromloo Design for his Mexico City apartment. He wanted a place to host family and friends, as well as comfortable, inspiring accommodation to offer visiting artists. Given the flexibility to indulge her creative licence, Jessica wanted the apartment to complement the exuberance of downtown Mexico City.

Located in a converted 1940s office building, the original one-bedroom apartment was bland and boxy. The brief included adding a second bedroom for guests and reducing the size of the kitchen to make space for a second bathroom. Jessica broke the boxy layout by enclosing the new bedroom with a curved wall, which had a knock-on effect for the rest of the design. 'This floor plan allowed us to be more creative and whimsical,' Jessica says.

The entrance hall shimmers with gold chain sconces reflecting in the mirrored wall and a dazzling pattern of tiles that morph into the kitchen. Here, the blue and yellow palette is inspired by the Frida Kahlo Museum (aka Blue House or Casa Azul), and the shapeshifting geometries enhance the mesmerising effect.

Blue and yellow tiles meet terracotta, grey and white beneath the dining table. These pave the main path through the apartment, pieced together with expanses of cork flooring that ground the sofa and beds. Jessica looked to the church across the road for the terracotta hue, and to other historical buildings in the area for the wavy detail used for the wainscoting and curtain stitching.

Splashes of bright red and cobalt blue are repeated through the apartment, on doors, thresholds and walls. 'Because there is a lot going on, these coloured elements connect the dots and make it feel cohesive,' Jessica explains. Similarly, green appears in the avocado-coloured custom sideboard, inspired by a visit to Diego Rivera and Frida Kahlo's studios, and in the main bedroom, where it is spliced with pink.

Jessica imaginatively repurposed an antique door she found in a store in Puebla as the headboard, as she did with other finds from the local La Lagunilla flea market. Dragon-shaped sconces support a kitchen shelf and salvaged ironwork attributed to mid-century designer Arturo Pani forms a decorative back to the modular sofa. Add to these an eclectic mix of designer pieces sourced from vintage dealers in Mexico and Los Angeles, including Pedro Friedeberg's hand chair, Isamu Noguchi's coffee table, a writing desk painted by David Serrano and a mosaic-topped 1960s dining table.

The bathroom, in contrast, is an ethereal space while still playful and expressive. The pared-back palette exudes a serene and calming quality, while mirrored panels repurposed as cabinet fronts reflect the light from the vintage pendants and pineapple wall sconce.

This patchwork of colour, pattern and objects animates this pied-à-terre with life and vitality. By embodying the energy and eclecticism of the streets, it transforms the apartment into an intriguing source of creative inspiration and discovery.

174

Previous page: The apartment is an eclectic mix of modern, vintage, designer and repurposed furniture and objects.

Right: A dazzling pattern of concrete tiles by Rayito de Sol paves the floor in the entry, kitchen, dining and circulation areas. The same pattern is used for the wall, which is painted to create a morphing effect.

Ayromloo Design

Above: Gold chain sconces in the entry are created using copper plates from
the La Lagunilla flea market.

Above: Traditional architecture, like that seen through the living room window, inspired many of the apartment details. Jessica sourced the Pedro Friedeberg hand chair and Noguchi coffee table (with marble top) from vintage store Trouvé in Mexico City.

Following page: Jessica sourced the French mosaic dining table and Allan Gould chairs from vintage store Downtown20 in Los Angeles, and the French deco bar cabinet from vintage store Trouvé in Mexico City. The repurposed dragon sconces support the kitchen shelf.

Kaleidoscopic Collage

Ayromloo Design

'The floor plan is somewhat complicated, but also geometrically pure. Taking pure geometry, rearranging it differently, adding playful colour and pattern, I think this is what postmodern design does.'

Jessica Ayromloo, founder
and designer, Ayromloo Design

Ayromloo Design

Previous page: The guest bedroom is enclosed by a curved wall, with cobalt blue framing the threshold.
Left: An antique door has been repurposed into a bedhead, and a Casamidy lantern hangs over the vintage Drexel side table.

Above, left to right: Jessica picked up the bathroom mirror, ceiling light and mirrored panels on the vanity at the local flea market; Also in the main bedroom is a painted writing desk by David Serrano from Downtown20.

184

FURNITURE WITH DYNAMISM

~~~

Designer: Mario Milana
Location: New York, United States

Growing up in Milan in the 1980s and 1990s, Mario Milana was at the epicentre of Italian design and artisanal production. His father designed exhibition systems for pavilions and fairs, and Mario was surrounded by architects and designers. 'There was just so much creativity everywhere. I think it's something that you feel by osmosis,' Mario says. He studied industrial design in Milan and interned with Denis Santachiara, and then moved to New York where he worked as a senior designer for Karim Rashid before establishing his own eponymous practice in 2014.

Synthesising these experiences, Mario designs furniture that is driven by function and infused with a sense of magic and surprise. He embeds dynamism into the form to provide greater comfort – this interaction elicits a reaction from users while the correlative elements create an expressive composition. 'I'm not looking to create something stereotypically beautiful, but something that people remember, to create that connection and that smile,' he says.

His first chair, a brasserie dining chair named DePostura, has two geometric elements for the seat and back, assembled on a sinuous steel frame. The high back is designed to hang a jacket or coat, the three-way bend in the structure creates a spring for lumbar support and the articulated backrest is adjustable in height. 'You have a dynamic and constant interaction with the piece. It invites you to assume a certain position so that you are more engaged with your body and comfortable in the long run,' Mario explains.

He adapted the design of DePostura to create the Rulla rocking chair. Two wooden spheres on the base serve as footrests, and the rolls of leather offcuts on the frame that provide a comfortable headrest are the result of Mario's desire to reuse waste. Made by artisanal manufacturers in Milan, his furniture fuses traditional craftsmanship and contemporary design, and showcases the hand of the maker and patina of materials.

The Masand also offers dynamism that instils it with unexpected functionality. Conceived while on a meditation retreat in India, the Masand is inspired by the traditional bolster cushion. At first glance, the series of cylinders seem to form a padded bench or chaise longue, but with a simple adjustment, they can be moved to provide a backrest, headrest or leg support that gives the Masand a wave-like form. 'I like inviting interactivity and awareness. Maybe the way you're interacting with the piece or the way you are present in that moment. Something that brings you back in your place and makes you feel aware and engaged in whatever is happening', says Mario.

While form follows function in Mario's work, there is expression and interaction that elevates that form into a fresh, surprising and distinctive composition. 'It's the fun part of it that is still there, I think, in the Milanese tradition,' he says.

185

Left, clockwise: DePostura chair; Rulla rocking chair; Masand. Photographer: Davide Milana

FEEL-GOOD VIBES

~~~

Designer: Merve Kahraman Design Studio
Project name: Bebek Residence
Location: Istanbul, Turkey

Photographer: Ozan Bal

When Merve Kahraman, founder of Merve Kahraman Design Studio, designed the first apartment for her client in New York, she used a Scandinavian-inspired palette with natural and neutral tones and materials, based on her client's request. But for the second apartment, this time in Istanbul, Merve upped the ante with more colours, patterns and custom furnishings to create a lively pied-à-terre that conjures a cafe vibe.

The owner wanted to spend more time in her home country of Turkey when the pandemic hit in 2020. While she initially preferred naturals, pastels and black and white, Merve encouraged her to be more adventurous. 'I wanted to introduce her to vibrant energetic colours because it was a depressing time. Colour can really help our psychology and create an uplifting environment,' says Merve.

Bebek Residence faces a large park and has views of lush green trees and clear blue skies. Merve brought these colours inside with a dark-green sofa and pastel blue walls that blend the interior with nature. The original mirrored wall reflects the living room and outdoors to create the illusion of greater light and space. Despite its small size, this multifunctional room offers a variety of areas for the owner to enjoy, including a sofa, dining banquette, reading nook, piano and balcony. 'The concept was to create diversity by designing multiple spaces in this fresh and cosy apartment.'

She designed nearly all the furniture and lighting for the apartment, or used and adapted items from her product collection. Merve's approach to furniture mediates art and design, fusing her desire for self-expression and the need to meet a client's functional requirements. Creating bespoke furniture is also part of Merve's sustainable approach to design. The idea is that it encourages clients to develop a more personal bond with their belongings and home. 'It's nicer to have something you create memories with so that you keep them or pass them to your children,' she explains.

Merve draws inspiration from a myriad of sources, including Turkish culture, the Italian Radicals, mid-century American design and the desire to create a sense of nostalgia. Her Abide coffee table, with its modern interpretation of the evil eye symbol, holds court in the centre of the living room. 'It's like a talisman for the house,' Merve says. The amorphous-shaped table is made with three different types of marble, and the legs are wrapped with a classic chequered fabric designed by Alexander Girard for Maharam in the 1970s. The same fabric is also on the N-Gene armchair, teamed with leather and cane. The chair is a re-envisioning of one that Merve's uncle, Engin, designed in the 1970s, and she named it for him.

A dining banquette nestled into the corner of the room is styled like a cafe, with a pastel-pink leather seat and carefully curated artwork and objects adorning the walls and colourful terrazzo bookshelf. In keeping with the black-and-white patterning, the timber dining table has handcrafted black-and-white marble legs, and the custom Gina stools have the same black-and-white chequers and are designed like a mini celestial throne.

Next to the living room is the client's favourite spot – a quiet reading nook with a bright red-and-white striped daybed and faux awning above. Merve also designed a piano stool upholstered with plush velvet, and a shoe storage credenza made with wood veneer using a traditional marquetry technique. The handcrafted wallpaper in the guest bathroom also has nostalgic cafe vibes, and the two peacocks are strategically placed to reflect in the clear arch of the two-tone mirror, creating an illusion of a bower.

Designed at a time when the world needed uplifting, Bebek Residence is a calm and happy space with fresh, feel-good vibes. It reflects Merve's love of colour and fondness for nostalgia, and she proudly says that her client now really loves colour too.

Previous page: The dining banquette surrounded by a curated display of artworks from a poster company contributes to the cafe atmosphere of the apartment.

Right: Merve's Cassini floor lamp is inspired by the Cassini–Huygens mission – a collaboration between NASA, the European Space Agency, and the Italian Space Agency.

Merve Kahraman Design Studio

190

Merve Kahraman Design Studio

Previous page: The mirrored wall reflects the living room, with the Abide coffee table and N-Gene armchair in the foreground.
Left: Merve custom-designed the dining table, banquette, Gina stools, terrazzo bookshelf and mint-green Ziron chandelier.

Above, left to right: The apartment faces the adjacent park; The Rayaz credenza is made with wood veneer using a traditional marquetry technique.

Merve Kahraman Design Studio

'We have many different colours and shapes in nature, so it feels more natural to have many different colours and shapes inside, rather than an all-white or all-neutral space.'

Merve Kahraman, founder and designer,
Merve Kahraman Design Studio

Merve Kahraman Design Studio

Previous page: In the powder room, the arched mirror has two different tints, and the peacocks on the wallpaper are reflected in the lighter arch.

Above, left to right: The Abide side table is also in the bedroom; The quiet reading nook has blue stucco painted walls and red-and-white striped seating, pillows and faux awning.
Right: A piano with custom-made velvet pouf is in the entrance.

Feel-Good Vibes

SOVIET
SENTIMENT

~~~

Designer: Mistovia
Project name: Katowice
Location: Katowice, Poland

Photographer: ONI Studio

The city of Katowice in Poland has a strong modernist legacy. The minimalist, functionalist style was ripe for the city's intensive development before World War II, and in the 1960s and 1970s it provided the foundation for the large-scale residential buildings and civic developments that came to define Soviet-era architecture. While the apartments may be identical and nondescript from the outside, the vibrant interior of this small apartment surprises and delights. Designer Marcin Czopek of Mistovia took the modernist origins and 1970s ambience of the existing flat as his starting point, and dialled it up with bright colour, chunky terrazzo and the imaginative repurposing of vintage furniture. 'The use of daring colours was somewhat of an extension of the climate we found in the flat upon starting with our client, and we wished to showcase the possibility of juxtaposing completely different materials,' says Marcin.

200

The clients – a young couple – engaged Mistovia to create a practical, memorable short-term rental that would stop online scrollers in their tracks. Marcin embraced the challenge of creating a fresh and functional space within their tight budget. 'There are so many apartments in Poland from the 1970s. Unfortunately, young people often get rid of the fit-out completely. We wanted to refer to the history and atmosphere of the existing interior,' he explains.

The 35-square-metre apartment is located on the eleventh floor with views to the centre of Katowice. Marcin removed walls to convert the two-room apartment into an open-plan room for living, cooking, dining and sleeping, creating the illusion of a larger space. The bathroom is enclosed with glass blocks that allow light to filter in, and one wall of the flat has been stripped back to the structural concrete, exposing a roughly textured and neutral-coloured backdrop for materials, colours and furnishings.

Different floor surfaces provide subtle spatial definition. Timber flooring fosters a feeling of calm in the living and bedroom area, and chunky terrazzo tiles inject graphic vibrancy into the dining area and kitchenette. 'The tiles draw on the trend of terrazzo dating back to Poland's communist times,' says Marcin. Terrazzo continues on the floor and walls of the bathroom, with darker tones and larger stones. And while the glass blocks of the bathroom hail from modernist origins and are inspired by the building's stairwell, they certainly saw a revival in the 1980s, becoming an iconic characteristic of architecture of the time.

Sleek, reflective materials contrast with rough and matte surfaces. The stainless steel sideboard adds an industrial edge and the mirrored cupboard next to the kitchen enhances the light and sense of space. Bursts of colour tie in with the terrazzo tiles, such as an intensely blue bathroom door made of stained plywood, a red-velvet tubular headboard and a brick-red curtain that wraps around the glass blocks to separate the bedroom and bathroom.

The previous owner left perfectly conserved furniture in the apartment, and Marcin creatively repurposed it to serve new functions: the chest of drawers from the living room is now a kitchen cupboard, and a sideboard is now a television unit and storage. 'They were polished to the point of shining, no doubt from when the block of flats was constructed.' The original black power points and light fixtures have also been retained and showcased to embrace the legacy of design.

Previous page: The exposed concrete wall provides a backdrop to the living room. A sideboard left in the apartment has been repurposed into the television unit and storage.

Right: Terrazzo flooring is used for the dining, kitchen and bathroom, and timber for the bed and living area.
Following page: The kitchen cupboard is repurposed from a chest of drawers, and the bentwood chairs are by Paged.

Mistovia

202

Mistovia

'When I went to art school, my painting style was colourful abstractions: connections of rounded forms with simple geometrical ones. When choosing my studies, interior architecture seemed to me more of an artistic direction than architecture. It seems to me that my "inner" painting is clearly visible in my projects. I look at them more like a canvas.'

Marcin Czopek,
founder and designer, Mistovia

Previous page: Marcin sourced the crystal glass ceiling lamp from the vintage store Szpeje in Krakow.
Above: The basin is offset on the vanity to provide surface space.

Right: The bathroom door is blue-stained plywood, and the graphic and chunky terrazzo tiles are designed by Luigi Romanelli for Fioranese.

SUBVERSIVE SCENERY

~~~~~

Designer: Puntofilipino
Project name: Apartment Milano
Location: Milan, Italy

Photographer: Polina Parcevskya

The owners of this Milan apartment love art and design and they had a clear aesthetic direction for Puntofilipino. They wanted the architectural character maintained, to feel a connection to nature, to have furniture inspired by the Memphis Group and Pop Art, and to feel as if they lived in an impressionist landscape painting. Puntofilipino looked to Italy's long and varied artistic legacy, drawing on the frescoed interiors of Venetian palaces, the glamour of art deco and the vibrant aesthetics of Pop Art and Memphis to create immersive spaces with a theatrical scenographic effect. 'We wanted to break with the aesthetic minimalism that currently prevails, and to achieve a space of radical and scandalous sensibility,' says interior designer Gema Gutiérrez, founder of Puntofilipino. The design both respects and subverts the period interiors to create a contemporary home that inspires the imagination.

The original spaces of the apartment – formerly a retail and repair shop for vintage lamps – have been restored, and the walls adorned with imagery and motifs evocative of other times and places. 'We worked with innovative materials that are respectful of the environment and reminiscent from another era, and took an elegant and daring approach to the colour palette that is in line with the aesthetic of Italian palaces,' says Gema.

A mural of moody, dense forest envelops the living and dining room, providing a relaxed environment and bucolic backdrop that offers a metaphorical connection to nature. Puntofilipino studied the variations of light and colour in the room to ensure the image captured the movement and life of an impressionist landscape painting. The wallcovering slips over the cornices for visual continuity, and the natural imagery and colours provide a soft and traditional contrast to the strong and unusual geometric forms of the furnishings and lighting.

Three arched openings lead to the kitchen, bathroom and bedroom, each framed with a swirling pattern that evokes the veining of Cipollino marble. Marble is embedded in the culture of Italian architecture, and the swirling marble-inspired ceramic material is a common thread through the apartment, embellishing the kitchen walls, splashback, benchtop and bedhead. In the kitchen, it is layered with a band of vertical tiles and deep terracotta-coloured bio-concrete mosaics. 'The colours and materials taken separately can seem very outrageous, but the combination creates visual impact,' says Gema. The layering of colour and materials animates the walls with a panelled effect and the cornices are painted white to highlight the separation and ornamental detail between the walls and ceiling.

The bedroom floor is patterned with large pebble-like forms, like oversized terrazzo, while the bathroom is adorned with a luxe wallcovering of gold fan motifs, recalling art deco, for which much inspiration was drawn from ancient Egyptian tombs and temples. 'We wanted to represent the frescoes and paintings on classical walls in an updated way, and to present the bathroom to resemble the concept of a temple.'

Simultaneously radical and serene, the subversive and picturesque design of this apartment provides a rich backdrop to life and transports your imagination to other times and places while offering contemporary living in the heart of Milan.

Previous page: Surfaces are wholly covered through the apartment, including the arched opening between the kitchen and the dining/living room.

Right: The landscape wallpaper Bellagio by Glamora provides a scenic backdrop to the dining area, which features table and chairs from Da A Italia.

211

Puntofilipino

Left, top left and right: Puntofilipino use a sideboard from Da A Italia for the kitchen cabinetry, and layered the walls a variety of materials: swirling Policroma from Florim, striped ceramics from Fornace Brioni, bio-concrete tiles made from Japanese knotweed and shells from American signal crayfish.

Bottom left: The Bonhomme floor lamp from Atelier Areti and Jack shelving from B&B Italia are strong geometric forms against the naturalistic backdrop Following page: The living area is light and airy with furniture from Santa & Cole and Saba Italia.

'We wanted to break with the aesthetic minimalism that currently prevails, and to achieve a space of radical and scandalous sensibility. Italian design is daring, groundbreaking and does not ask permission to be displayed.'

Gema Gutiérrez, founder, creative director
and designer, Puntofilipino

214

216

Puntofilipino

Previous page and above: The swirling, marble-inspired wallcovering continues in the bedroom, where the floor is tiled with a pebble-like pattern.

Right: The wallcovering Luxury by Inkiostro Bianco evokes a glamorous art deco atmosphere in the bathroom.

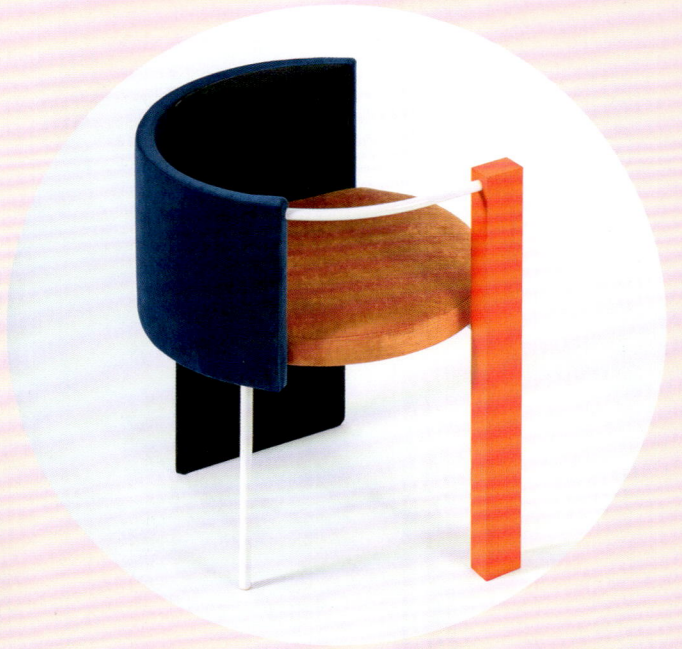

AVANT-GARDE FURNITURE

~

Designer: Supaform
Location: Milan, Italy

Form follows emotion for artist and designer Maxim Scherbakov, founder of Milan-based creative studio Supaform. He works across furniture, interiors, painting, sculpture and digital art, and explores the interplay of these disciplines to create surprising spaces and functional art pieces. 'I'm an artist, and then a designer. I prefer to rely on feelings and intuition more than on calculation and business approach,' Maxim says.

Maxim studied painting and interior design at university in Saint Petersburg, inheriting the values of the revolutionary avant-garde who shaped the suprematism and constructivism movements. He has also been a street artist, involved in skateboarding and street culture, while continuing his painting and work in architectural and furniture design. 'This rebellious and daring energy of subculture has influenced me and helped me to combine my classical art education with contemporary subculture vision,' he says.

The influence of the avant-garde is alive and well in the Apart chair, which is inspired by and dedicated to the water tower building in St Petersburg designed by constructivist architect Yakov Chernikhov in 1931. The Apart chair is an asymmetric collision of individual elements in different shapes, colours and materials that evokes the form of the water tower. Like the avant-garde's work, it has strong, active colour and explores abstract forms and space. 'I love when the piece has a strong concept with a little bit of easiness and inconsistence. It's important for me to be in the middle of irony and seriousness. The beauty and ugliness, the commonness and fancy luxury. All these things are part of my interest.'

The New Normative armchair also has an asymmetric composition. It is part of a larger collection conceived from Maxim's visualisation of a fantasy reality in which modernism had not forced out neoclassicism. 'Under such circumstances, the furniture would remain normative and would not lose its originality and uniqueness at the same time,' he says. It speaks to his interest in retrofuturism, a creative movement that depicts a future envisioned from the past. The armchair has a fluted wooden pedestal, like a classical column, for the base, and the coffee table is wrapped with an intricately carved decorative frieze often seen in Soviet-era building entrances.

One of the recent Supaform collections is Hidden Entourage, which, like postmodernism, subverts the idea that form follows function and that furniture is merely utilitarian. Each piece has a bold, sculptural shape that is functional, yet limited in that function: chairs are uncomfortable, tables have rippled surfaces. It showcases Maxim's philosophy and approach of emotion first, utility second, as he creates a compromise between art and design. 'Once we stop expecting day-to-day objects to serve us, once we agree to let go of total control over them, they shine with pure emotion and undeniable beauty that does not need a reason.'

Left, clockwise: New Normative armchair; Apart chair; Hidden Entourage Collection. Photographer: Serena Eller

RED HOT

~~~

Architect/designer: SCEG Architects
Project name: Folie Falò
Location: Claviere, Italy

Photographer: Barbara Corsico

Postmodern designers believed in the power of objects and materials as vehicles for storytelling and sensory communication. That idea burns at the heart of Folie Falò where a fiery red veneer that greets you as you enter injects a sense of warmth and heat into this home, like a glowing fire. Fusing function and feeling, it marks the places for the family to sit, sleep and gather, and is the leading character in this narrative-driven design.

Folie Falò is in a mountain chalet in northern Italy. It is the second home of Eirini Giannakopoulou and Stefano Carera of SCEG Architects. While the instinctual approach to small-footprint design is to use light and neutral tones to enhance the sense of space, SCEG took a pragmatic and poetic approach with a design inspired by the alpine landscape and tradition.

The entrance opens to the kitchen, dining and living room, where the sofa folds out to a bed. The bathroom and storage are in the centre of the apartment, alongside the hallway, and there is a small room at the back with two stacked double beds. 'Having to deal with the size of the niche and height of the apartment, which is also minimal, the intuition was to create a mix between the Japanese tatami and the classic bunk bed,' says Eirini.

The red veneer, designed by Sottsass for ALPI in the early 1980s, forms the surfaces of the dining bench, sofa backrest, bedheads and corridor console. Plastics and veneers became a signature material of the objects produced by both Studio Alchimia and Memphis, and their unconventional use of laminates in furniture changed the face of contemporary design. Coloured and patterned veneer offered possibilities for transforming furniture into an expression of communication. In Folie Falò, the intense red veneer, with its hypnotic woodgrain veining, is a hot burst of colour highlighting the furniture pieces and gathering places in each room.

SCEG tempered the red with natural colours of deep blue and light blue-green, and edged the joinery with brass for a metallic sheen. Shades of pink infuse playfulness into the palette – the delicate pink and dusty grey in the kitchenette, and the pink frame of the bunk bed and ladder that curves as it merges with the wall. This curve softens the edges of all the joinery, as well as the hallway ceiling, wall panelling, bathroom mirror and dining table.

Every decorative element in the apartment is also aligned with the mountain story and atmosphere. 'There are references to the woods and alps in the decorative objects, and the vertical wooden handles on cupboard doors refer to the trees that surround the house,' Stefano says. The decorative references have a fairy tale quality, with floral patterns on the splashback and soft furnishings, a print of Enzo Mari's *La Rana (The Frog)* poster and Philippe Starck's Gnome stool, used here as a side table.

In Folie Falò, the colour palette and decorative pairings of modern and traditional contribute to a narrative in line with the apartment's alpine location.

Previous page: The red veneer, designed by Ettore Sottsass in the early 1980s, injects warmth and colour into this small mountain home.

Right: The sofa doubles as a bed, with the joinery incorporating a side table and shelving above.
Following page: Two stacked doubled beds are cleverly tucked into a small room, with the 'forest' bedding contributing to the alpine narrative.

SCEG Architects

Red Hot

'We like to imagine a "movie" –
a sequence of never-predictable
scenes. The element of surprise,
the unpredictable, is a very
important element in our projects.'

Stefano Carera and Eirini Giannakopoulou,
founders and architects, SCEG Architects

227

Above, clockwise: The Attila Gnome stool by Philippe Starck for Kartell in the living room; The golden-coloured seats of the Claretta chairs from Miniforms tie in with the metallic trim of the bench seat; A crafted advent calendar adds to the character of the apartment.

Right: The view through the hallway to the dining area, where furnishings are designed to maximise space.

230

Above: The metallic trim and light blue-green hue is continued in the bathroom, paired with dusty pink cabinetry and tiles from Ceramica Vogue.

Right: The kitchen is designed as a self-contained element, with grey and dusty pink cabinetry. The ceiling light from Oluce continues the gold trim.

Red Hot

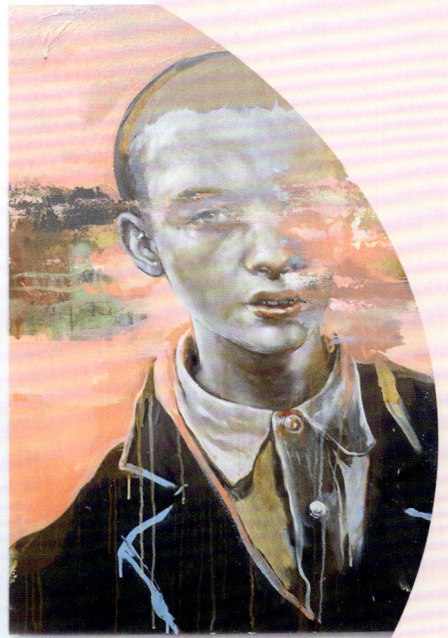

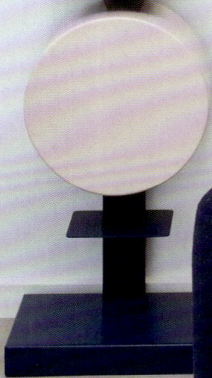

ANIMATING ACCESSIBILITY

~~~

Architect/designer: Sibling Architecture
Project name: Frenches Interior
Location: Melbourne, Australia

It is rare to find an imaginative approach to accessibility in architecture. Accessibility is often about meeting minimum utilitarian requirements, such as countertop heights, door widths, wheelchair turning circles or grab bars. But why not be creative and a little quirky? Exploring new ways of designing for accessibility and inclusiveness, Sibling Architecture injected playfulness, whimsy and Memphis-inspired motifs into Frenches Interior in Melbourne.

The clients assist people who have experienced significant physical or cognitive injuries and they wanted to reflect and facilitate this in their home and office. A high level of accessibility was also vital for their friends who are wheelchair users. Sibling adapted the interior to serve as a home and workplace and designed custom furniture to enrich everyone's experience and social interactions. 'The clients wanted something special and gave us creative free rein,' says architect Jane Caught.

Flexibility is embedded into the interior with spaces and furniture that can be reconfigured to suit different users and uses. The clients' workplace is at the front of the house, where sheer curtains conceal sitting and standard desks, and a table with deep tubular pockets holds pens, plants and flowers, and champagne and crostini for after work.

The living room is inspired by the home of Gertrude Stein and Alice B. Toklas in 1930s Paris, where avant-garde writers and artists such as F. Scott Fitzgerald, Ernest Hemingway, Pablo Picasso and Henri Matisse would gather in the salon on Saturday evenings. To promote this convivial, inclusive atmosphere, Sibling designed a custom couch comprising ten triangular modules, like cake slices. Together, the modules form a circle, or they can break apart into a myriad of configurations. The slices can be moved to include wheelchair users in the seating arrangement and pink powder-coated handles help visitors to sit.

'We had been thinking about furniture that structures group dynamics in an egalitarian way. We were always imagining what a couch for eight people could look like, and this project was a lovely opportunity to materialise the idea,' says designer Timothy Moore.

Similarly, the circular dining table allows for easier circulation and inclusive seating, and the solid terrazzo lazy Susan assists accessibility. The circular motif throughout the furniture – seat backs, noticeboards, cushions, side tables and bedhead – is also used as a symbol of inclusion and sharing.

A strong Memphis influence is evident in the squiggly tubes of the tables and in the totems, which hold some of the clients' valued possessions. Composed of stacked geometric forms, one totem has perforated cupboards that store bottles of whiskey, while a series of three totems in the library displays prized art books.

The colour and material palette adds to the fun and whimsy. Bright orange and deep pink are tempered with navy, blushed pink and peach, and a variety of textural qualities juxtapose hard and soft surfaces. The wobbly tubes holding up terrazzo or glass tabletops are coloured with chrome automotive paint, while metal chair frames have velvet-upholstered seats and perforated metal seat backs. Baby-pink faux fur cushions and dreamy white sheers soften the composition. The colour fades away in the bedroom upstairs, where the white tables, totems and bedhead promote calm and rest.

Animating accessibility in design, Sibling demonstrates how expressive forms and practical functionality can go hand in hand. One need not be sacrificed for the other; you can have your cake and eat it too.

234

Previous page: The squiggly table bases coloured with chrome automotive paint. Following page: The sofa has ten triangular modules that can be arranged in different configurations and to include wheelchair users. One seat has handles to help visitors sit and stand.

Right: The dining table has a solid terrazzo lazy Susan to aid accessibility. The metal frame chairs have velvet-upholstered seats and perforated metal seat backs.

'The main sensibility of Memphis
is their playfulness, the freedom of
their aesthetic and material choices.
Convention is out the window, and the
idea that one can define their own way
of living as opposed to conforming
to predictable inhabitations is very
refreshing and liberating.'

Timothy Moore, co-founder
and designer, Sibling Architecture

Sibling Architecture

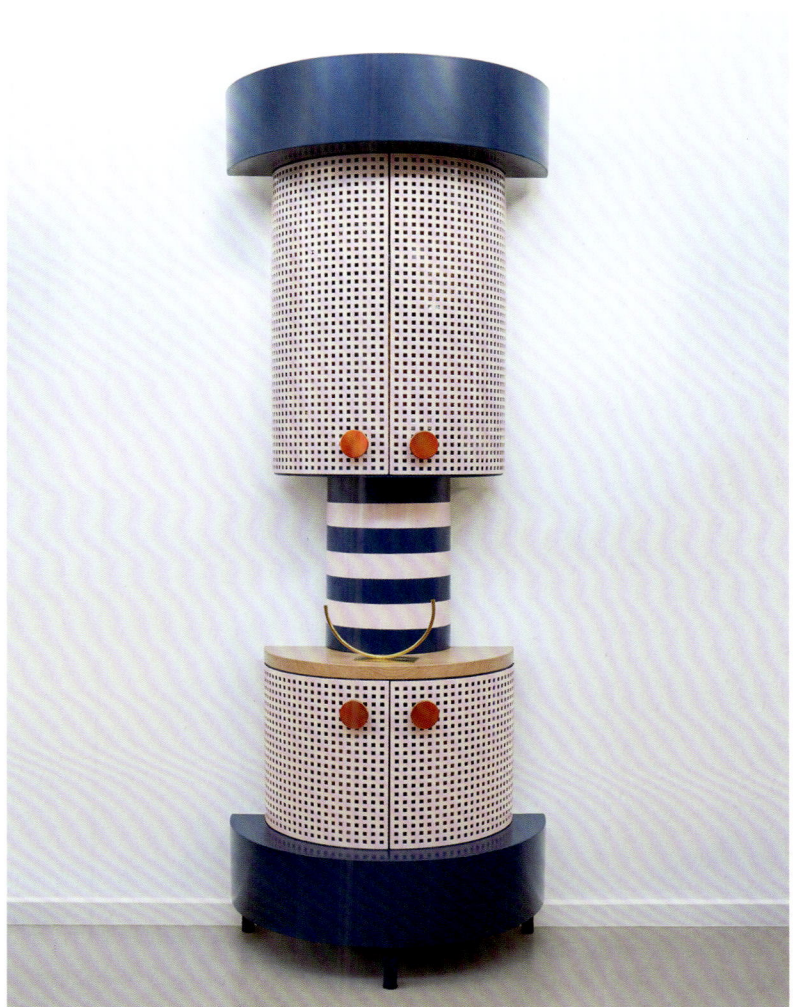

Previous page: Books are stacked vertically in totem-like shelving that incorporates geometric forms.
Left: The work area is surrounded by a sheer curtain and the table has deep tubular pockets to holds pens, plants, flowers and even champagne.

Above, left to right: In the bedroom, custom shelves and hooks are fixed to a structural wall lattice to provide storage and display of objects and art; Sibling designed storage in the form of a totem with stacked geometric forms and perforated cupboards.

HEART AND SOUL

~~~

Designer: Ash Dipert
Project name: California Bungalow
Location: Bakersfield, USA

Photographers: Jeran McConnel, Benjamin Rasmussen
Stylist: Jeran McConnel

This backyard bungalow is only 19 square metres, but it packs a punch beyond its diminutive size. Woodworker and furniture maker Ash Dipert transformed the three adjoining structures (a former pool pump house, changing room and unfinished bathroom) into a guest suite where colour, curves and character collide. Showcasing his craftsmanship skills, Ash custom designed and made nearly every element, imbuing the dwelling with heart and soul.

Located behind Ash's parents' Craftsman house in Bakersfield, California, the exterior of the bungalow is painted with simple geometric shapes that endow the small building with a big personality. A trompe l'oeil arch gives the illusion of a doorway, a circle rises in the gable like the sun, and three semicircles evoke a face, with a daybed for a tongue and a stained glass window for an ear.

The half-moon stained glass window, bought from a local antique shop, inspired the palette of pale pink, forest green, mustard and terracotta, as did Ash's upbringing in Papua New Guinea and Ghana and travels to Sri Lanka. 'In all those places, they tend to go as bright and as wild as they can with colour, and it always contrasts against green jungle and red earth,' Ash says. He also continued the semicircle shape of the window and its details throughout the interior, loving the challenge of crafting curves that also help to optimise circulation and space. 'I like things that are intentional and complicated and that people can see and appreciate the complexity,' he says.

The kitchen, living and sleeping areas are all combined in one room, for which Ash removed an interior wall. At less than 2.5 metres wide, the room had to be designed like a puzzle so that all the pieces fit while still leaving plenty of space. At the end of the room is the sofa and rainbow-painted Murphy bed, with four arched alcoves above for display, and a half-moon nook recessed into the wall for shelfs, mirroring the stained glass window. The kitchen joinery extends along the wall with curved ends to the cabinetry and pink terrazzo benchtop and custom semicircle brass handles.

Ash incorporated lots of clever storage solutions into the kitchen, including a pull-out shelf for the coffee machine and two pull-down compartments in the pink-tiled splashback for an induction cooktop and a knife block and cutting board. Along the opposite wall are two banquette-style seats, each with storage drawers underneath, and a corner seat that nestles into a tall painted arch that adjoins a narrow coat rack. The table on castors also has two semicircular forms for the base and marquetry timber top.

Geometric black-and-white tiles pave the floor and extend into the bathroom and changing room. The monochromatic stripes repeat the patterned circle on the exterior wall and provide a kaleidoscopic contrast to all the colourful curves.

The bathroom vanity is also curved, with a pink terrazzo benchtop, green cupboard doors and four brass handles that form a circle. With attention to detail and ingenuity, Ash inlaid a stained glass 'H' and 'C' into the brass shower knobs and made the whimsical U-shaped light fixture by repurposing a motorcycle exhaust pipe and adding marble and brass.

Every feature and detail within the bungalow serves a purpose and is cleverly designed and beautifully crafted to contribute to the playful personality of the space. That personality is continued on the exterior with an anthropomorphic face – the bungalow is like a colourful character in the backyard, smiling at the main house from across the pool.

Previous page: A Murphy bed folds down from the wall. Arched alcoves and a half-moon nook offer display and storage space.

Right: Ash painted the exterior with three semicircles (left) evoking a face, a circle rising in the gable like the sun, and a trompe l'oeil arch (right) that gives the illusion of a doorway.

Ash Dipert

Above: Concrete Collaborative made the Pacifica millennial pink retro mix terrazzo for the kitchen bench and bathroom vanity. The coffee machine is stored in an overhead cupboard with a pull-out shelf.

Right: Curved corners help optimise space in the small room, which neatly fits the sofa/bed, kitchen and dining/sitting area.

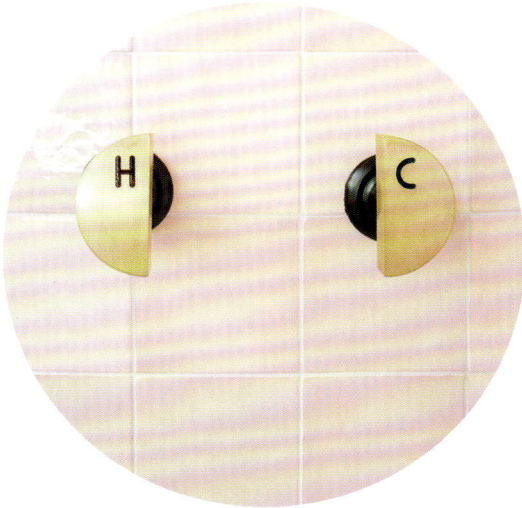

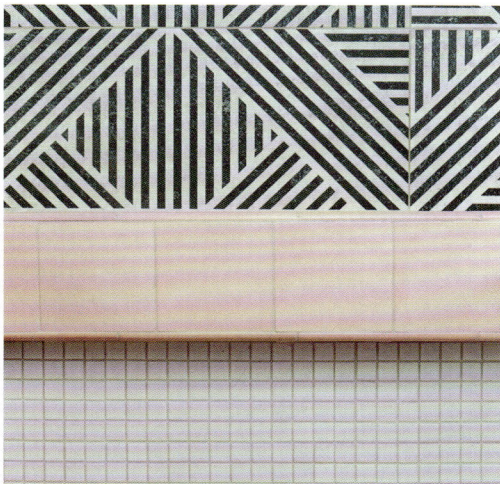

Left: Ash crafted all the furniture and joinery in the bungalow, including the curved green doors of the vanity and the light fixture made from marble, brass and a repurposed motorcycle exhaust.

Above, clockwise: Ash inlaid a stained glass 'H' and 'C' into the brass shower knobs; Mirrors and glass shower doors in the bathroom all have curves; Pink tiles mark the changes in the level of the floor, so they can be seen easily amid the geometric black-and-white floor tiles.

'In so much of the new modern designs, everything is 90-degree angles and sharp edges. It has no soul and the architecture has nothing that inspires me. So it comes back to more intention in the design, rather than just boxes that have doorways in them.'

Ash Dipert, designer,
woodworker and fabricator

251

Ash Dipert

Previous page: The banquette-style seats have storage drawers underneath, and the table has castors for easy movement.
Right: The changing room has existing bench seats that Ash painted and carved curves into the side of.

Above, left to right: The black-and-white circle on the exterior has the same geometric pattern as the tiles; Ash found the half-moon stained glass window at a local antique shop. It offers a view from the sofa/bed to the pool and the colours inspired the palette.

PLAYFUL
PERCEPTION

~~~~~

Architect/designer: Lake and Walls
Project name: Slavyansky Bulvar
Location: Moscow, Russia

Photographer: Oksana Zavarzina

Like Memphis, Lake and Walls believe that design does not have to be enduring, but it should be provocative, fresh and surprising. That is encapsulated in this Moscow apartment, in which every room has its own style and personality. It's a visual language that celebrates variety and vitality, and while each room is different, there is coherency in the diversity. 'Our clients are screenwriters for film. Their personal perception of the world is always diverse, depending on the picture they are working on. We transferred this perception into our design,' says architect Eugene Shevchenko of Lake and Walls.

The young couple engaged Lake and Walls to transform their 1970s apartment into a home for relaxation and work. Lake and Walls played with a cacophony of forms, colours, materials and furnishings to infuse the once-tired apartment with a cheerful mood and playfulness.

The living room is modern and stylish with comfortable, contemporary furniture and lighting. Mirrored surfaces framing the entry play with perception, and a wall of emerald-green and pale pink ceramic tiles introduces an unconventional material into the lounge, as does the vertical strip of stove tiles with colourful mythical imagery.

Pink and green continue in the hallway and the bedroom, where Lake and Walls added pistachio to the mix. 'The colour in this apartment is sensitive, contrasting and at the same time harmonious. But this is never on purpose, rather it is intuitive. The science of colour – it's not for us,' says designer Oksana Zavarzina. Black edging on the bedroom joinery accentuates the delineation of colour and form, like a two-dimensional drawing. The dark-green semicircle arching over the headboard, and the geometry of the handles and ceramic tiles in the nooks, also play with dimension and graphic effect.

Vibrant terrazzo floor tiles paving the hallway tie in the winsome pastels and intense bright hues that emanate throughout the apartment. Colour and function go hand in hand in the kitchen with the application of blue and red – cold and hot colours – directly corresponding to use: blue for the cupboards and red for the semicircular apron and cube-shaped rangehood. The dark purple extractor pipe blends the two, and the black-and-white speckled benchtop serves as a neutral. Tucked into the window is a small and sweet breakfast area with pale pink walls, a built-in planter and a table set on glass blocks to lighten the volume and make it airier.

Colours intensify in the bathroom and laundry where the vivacious palette bursts with joy. Bright turquoise is teamed with violet and yellow, while decorative timber drawers add character, warmth and comfort. The office is more subdued, with cork walls providing a soft and calming environment for the work of writers, as well as a convenient surface to pin up notes and ideas. Timber joinery provides separation between the two desks, and the raised floor is tiled with a black-and-white geometric pattern.

As with the colour and materials, Lake and Walls selected the furniture and lighting intuitively, incorporating modern, traditional, antique and expressive pieces. 'There was nothing forced, and all rules were discarded. We chose those that we felt a connection between colour, shape and surface,' says Oksana.

Indeed, this theme reigns throughout the apartment, with each room designed as an individual environment while also being part of the whole. 'Contrast and surprise form the basis of harmony. It's like yin and yang, somewhere in the middle of beauty, completely elusive,' says Eugene.

256

Previous page: The Hand Chair R by Versmissen is both a functional office chair and an expressive art piece – appropriate for two writers.

Right: The living room has green-tiled walls and a vertical strip of stove tiles down one edge.

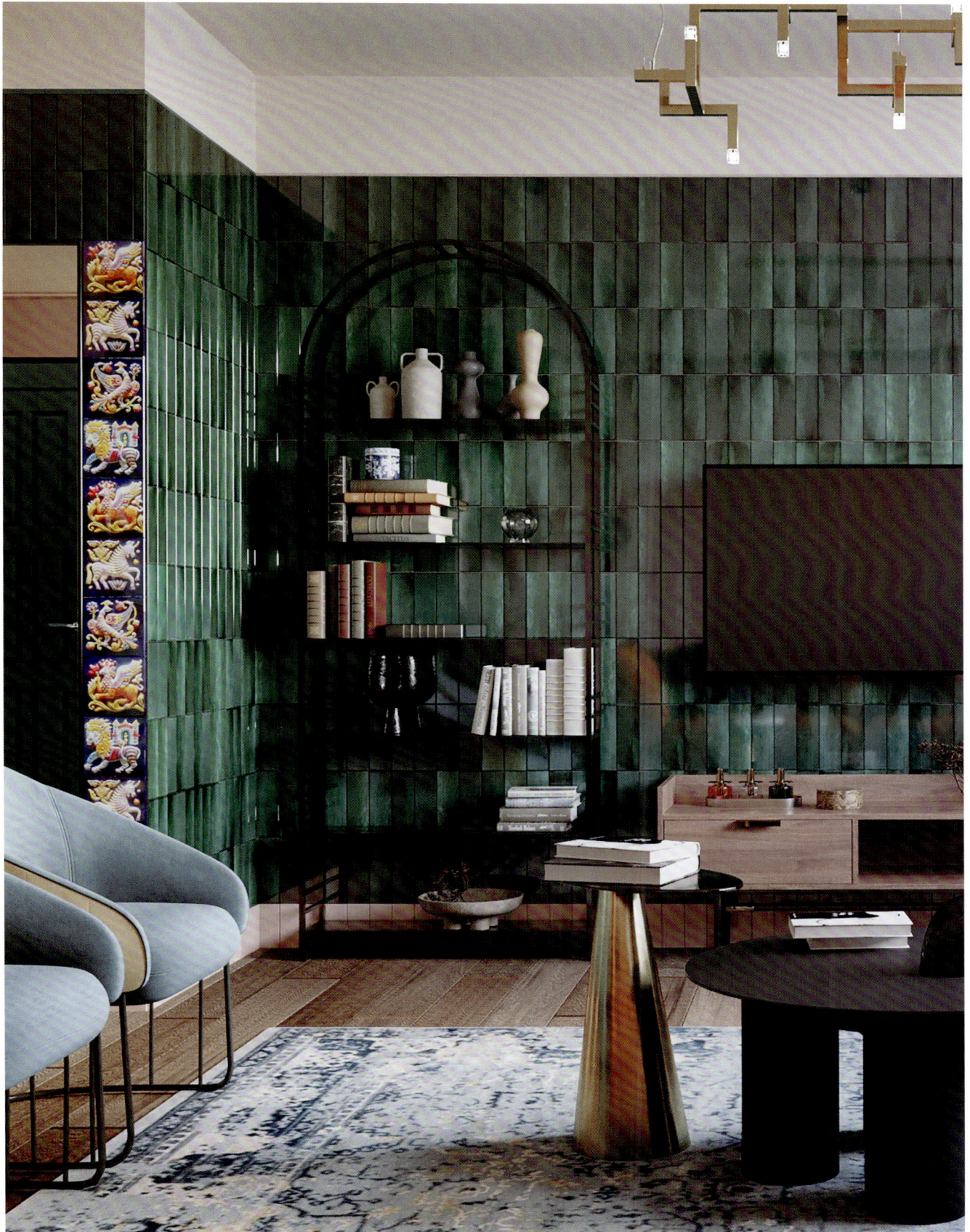

Lake and Walls

Above: The kitchen is colour-coded. Blue is used for the cupboards and red indicates the heat of the apron and rangehood.

Above: The pale pink breakfast area at the end of the kitchen has a built-in planter and glass blocks beneath the bench.

Following page: Black edging on the bedroom joinery accentuates its design, creating the look of a two-dimensional drawing. Tiled nooks provide bedside storage.

Lake and Walls

Above, left to right: Cork walls in the office are a convenient surface for pinning up notes and ideas; The entry hall has terrazzo flooring, and an antique cabinet stands outside the living area.

Above: The living room is furnished with contemporary pieces, including sofas and chairs from Sancal, coffee tables from La Forma, Bosa and Plust, and a chandelier from Versmissen.

Following page: The bathroom is bold and bright with yellow tiles and a purple sink and tapware set against turquoise walls and the terrazzo floor.

'There are as many styles as there are designers. It is very important for a designer to feel their own style. Whether they accept it or not, that is another question.'

Eugene Shevchenko and Oksana Zavarzina, founders, architect and designer, Lake and Walls

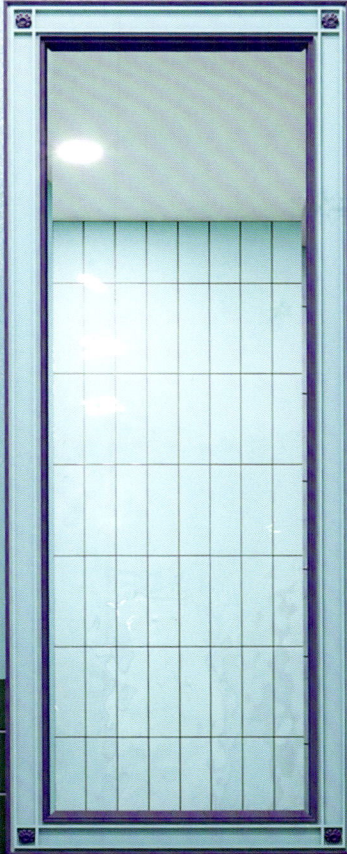

Architects and designers

2LG Studio
p. 132
London, United Kingdom
www.2lgstudio.com

Ash Dipert
p. 242
Bakersfield, United States
www.ashdipert.com

Ayromloo Design
p. 172
Los Angeles, United States
www.ayromloo.design

Chet Architecture
p. 146
Los Angeles, United States
www.chetarch.com

Fearon
p. 144
Gold Coast, Australia
www.fearon.shop

Fieldwork
p. 110
Melbourne, Australia
www.fieldworkprojects.com.au

Ghislaine Viñas
p. 146
New York, United States
www.ghislainevinas.com

Jassy
p. 160
New Orleans, United States

Lake and Walls
p. 254
Moscow, Russia
www.lakeandwalls.com

Marcante Testa
p. 62
Turin, Italy
www.marcante-testa.it

Mario Milana
p. 184
New York, United States
www.mariomilana.com

Marta Figueiredo
p. 50
Melbourne, Australia
www.marta-figueiredo.com

Mas Creations
p. 86
Valencia, Spain
www.mas-creations.com

Merve Kahraman Design Studio
p. 186
Istanbul, Turkey
www.mervekahraman.com

Mistovia
p. 198
Katowice, Poland
www.mistovia.com

Office S&M
p. 52
London, United Kingdom
www.officesandm.com

Owl Design
p. 12
London, United Kingdom
www.owldesign.co.uk

Point Supreme Architects
p. 100
Athens, Greece
www.pointsupreme.com

Puntofilipino
p. 208
Madrid, Spain
www.puntofilipino.com

SCEG Architects
p. 222
Turin, Italy
www.sceg.it

Sibling Architecture
p. 232
Melbourne, Australia
www.siblingarchitecture.com

Studio Ben Allen
p. 74
London, United Kingdom
www.studiobenallen.com

Studio Job
p. 120
Tilburg, Netherlands
www.studio-job.com

Studio Sam Buckley
p. 88
Edinburgh, United Kingdom
www.mrbuckley.co.uk

Supaform
p. 220
Milan, Italy
www.supaform.studio

WOWOWA
p. 38
Melbourne, Australia
www.wowowa.com.au

YSG
p. 26
Sydney, Australia
www.ysg.studio

266

Photographers

Alix McIntosh
p. 88–99
www.alixmcintosh.com

Annie Schlechter
p. 172–183, 268
www.annieschlechter.com

Barbara Corsico
p. 222–231
www.barbaracorsico.com

Benjamin Rasmussen
p. 242–253
www.benjaminrasmussenphoto.com

Carola Ripamonti
p. 62–73

Christine Francis
p. 232–241
www.christinefrancis.com

Davide Milana
p. 184

Efi Gousi
p. 100–109
www.efigousi.tumblr.com

French+Tye
p. 52–61, 74–85
www.frenchandtye.com

Garrett Rowland
p. 9, 146–159
www.garrettrowland.com

Jack Fearon
p. 144
www.fearon.shop

Jacqueline Marque
p. 160–171
www.jacquelinemarque.com

Jeran McConnel
p. 4, 242
www.oleanderandpalm.com

Jonathon Griggs
p. 6, 50
www.jonathongriggs.com

Jordan Malane
p. 144
www.jordanmalane.com

Kasia Gatkowska
p. 10, 120
www.kasiagatkowska.com

Martina Gemmola
p. 38–49
www.gemmola.com

Masquespacio
p. 86
www.masquespacio.com

Megan Taylor
p. 132–143
www.megantaylor.co.uk

Oksana Zavarzina
p. 254–265
www.lakeandwalls.com

ONI Studio
p. 198–207
www.oni.com.pl

Ozan Bal
p. 186–197
www.ozanbal.com

Polina Parcevskya
p. 208–219

Prue Ruscoe
p. 26–37
www.prueruscoe.com

Rachael Smith
p. 12–25, 271
www.rachaelsmith.net

Serena Eller
p. 220
www.serenaeller.com

Tom Ross
p. 110–119
www.tomross.xyz

Yannis Drakoulidis
p. 100–109
www.yannisdrakoulidis.com

268

Further reading

Didero, Maria Cristina, Evan Snyderman, Dennis Freedman, Deyan Sudjic & Catharine Rossi, *SuperDesign: Italian Radical Design 1965–75*, Monacelli Press, New York, 2017.

Farrell, Terry & Adam Nathaniel Furman, *Revisiting Postmodernism*, RIBA Publishing, Newcastle upon Tyne, 2017.

Gura, Judith, *Postmodern Design Complete*, Thames & Hudson, London, 2017.

Hopkins, Owen, *Postmodern Architecture: Less is a Bore*, Phaidon Press, London, 2020.

Jencks, Charles, *The Language of Post-Modern Architecture*, Rizzoli, New York, 1977.

Labaco, Ronald T, *Ettore Sottsass: Architect and Designer*, Merrell Publishers in association with Los Angeles County Museum of Art, London, 2006.

Radice, Barbara, *Memphis: Research, Experiences, Results, Failures, and Successes of New Design*, Thames and Hudson, London, 1984.

Venturi, Robert, *Complexity and Contradiction in Architecture*, Museum of Modern Art, New York, 1966.

Venturi, Robert, Denise Scott Brown & Steven Izenor, *Learning from Las Vegas*, MIT Press, Cambridge, 1972.

Artwork credits

9	Elliott Jerome Brown Jr, *Devin in Red Socks*, 2016
10	Mirrored sculpture by David Altmejd; Studio Job, *Rose Table*, 2005, marquetry of rosewood and coloured dyed through veneer, polished bronze feet; Rug: Studio Job for Nodus, *Perished Persian* (rug), 2009
21	Karel Balas, *Garden* (art print)
29	Billie Justice Thomson, *Coincidences*, 2016
30, 34	Murals by Lymesmith
41	Keith Haring, *Learning Through Art* (print), 1999
88	Florence Blanchard, *Wintergreen*
93	Will Martyr, *A Way With Words* (left) Florence Blanchard, *Wintergreen* (right)
113	Various artists throughout the project, including Justin Williams, Hana Shimada, Rhys Less, Carl Breitkreuz, Charlotte Ghaie and Andy Summons
120	David Altmejd, *Joy* (sculpture), 2020
123	Mirror sculpture by David Altmejd; Studio Job, *Rose Table*, 2005, marquetry of rosewood and coloured dyed through veneer, polished bronze feet; Studio Job for Nodus, *Perished Persian* (rug), 2009
126	David Hockney, *Vase and Flower* (etching); Studio Job, Cock Cross, 2010
127	Painting by Kara Walker; Studio Job, *Industry Cabinet*, 2009
129	David Altmejd sculpture; Studio Job table and Tour Eiffel lamp.
146	Mickalene Thomas, *Din Facing Forward*, 2012
149	Brett Murray, *Little Bubble*, 2014
151	AA Rucci, *Charlie's personal 'after school special' came at the hands and lips of his younger but wiser next-door neighbour Jill*, 2007
152	Paul Anthony Smith, *Untitled, Mask II*, 2019; Kehinde Wiley, *S. Francis of Adelaide* (bust), 2006; unknown painting
154	Derrick Adams, *Floater 24 (two floats)*
156–157	Mural by Adrian Kay Wong
160	Artwork by Sam Springston
179	Nick Farhi, *Blank Frosted Vessel*, 2019
196	Artwork by Enes Debran
197	Ahu Akgün, from the series '23 Seconds', 2017
198	LouLou Avenue for the Paper Collective, *Donnor*
208	Romina Ressia, *Coke* (photograph)
220	Paintings by Maxim Scherbakov
225	Enzo Mari, *La Rana* (poster), 1976
262	Photograph by Adriana Duque
263	Artwork by Paul Thurlby

269

Acknowledgements

Thank you to the architects, designers and photographers who made this book possible and gave us permission to publish your work.

Thank you to Paulina de Laveaux, Rachel Carter and the team at Thames & Hudson for bringing this book to life, Lorna Hendry for her expert copyediting and Claire Orrell for designing a stunning book.

Thanks to Professor Marilyn Cohen at Parsons School of Design for introducing me to postmodernism, and to Max Soans-Burne and Richard Burne of Max&You for introducing me to many of the furniture brands mentioned.

Thank you to my family and friends for all your support. And to the readers – I hope you enjoy it.

About the author

Rebecca L Gross is a Sydney-based writer who specialises in architecture, design and design history. She has a master's degree in the history of decorative arts and design from Parsons School of Design in New York and is interested in studying cultural history through the lens of architecture, design and visual culture.

Rebecca has been widely published in print and online media, including *Artichoke*, *Houses*, *Green* and *Sanctuary*, and writes for architecture practices and design studios.

Previous page: Mexico City Residence by Ayromloo (p. 172) Photographer: Polina Parcevskya

Right: Adventures in Space by Owl Design (p. 12) Photographer: Rachael Smith

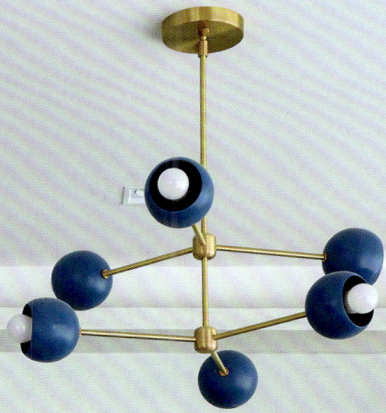